Darling Callum,
Let's aim for 10+ in 2016!
All my love,
Alison x

Tired of London, Tired of Life

TOM JONES

Tired of London, Tired of Life

TOM JONES

One thing a day to do in London

Virgin BOOKS

15

First published in the UK in 2012 by Virgin Books, an imprint of Ebury Publishing
A Random House Group Company

Copyright © Tom Jones, 2012

The author has asserted his right under the Copyright, Designs and Patents Act
1988 to be identified as the author of this work.

Every reasonable effort has been made to contact the copyright holders of material
reproduced in this book. If any have inadvertently been overlooked, the publishers
would be glad to hear from them and make good in future editions any errors or
omissions brought to their attention.

Address for companies within The Random House Group Limited can be found
at www.randomhouse.co.uk

The Random House Group Limited Reg. No. 954009

A CIP catalogue record for this book is available from the British Library

ISBN: 9780753540329

Design: Lottie Crumbleholme
Illustrations © Hannah Warren

Printed and bound in Italy by Printer Trento srl

To buy books by your favourite authors and register for offers, visit
www.randomhouse.co.uk

CONTENTS

For Cynthia

ACKNOWLEDGEMENTS

With thanks to Sue, Pete, Steve and Cynthia Jones for not telling me if they thought this was a silly idea, Jemima Warren for listening, Ronnie Whittington, Alison Gregory, Pete Winn and Jon Searle for coming on days out, Ruth Scott for allowing me space to work and Graeme Holloway for my desk.

Thanks also to Matt Brown, Lindsey Clarke, Jane Parker, Ian Mansfield, Daniel Shore, Samuel Johnson and everyone who shares their thoughts on London.

Finally, and above all, thanks to Hannah Knowles, Nicola Barr, Lottie Crumbleholme, Hannah Warren and Virgin Books for making this a reality.

'When a man is tired of London, he is tired of life ... for there is in London all that life can afford.'

DR SAMUEL JOHNSON, 1777

INTRODUCTION

When Samuel Johnson told James Boswell 'when a man is tired of London, he is tired of life … for there is in London all that life can afford', the year was 1777. Much of London was open countryside, and the population was a fraction of what it is today, but Johnson had already seen its potential.

Today, the city covers over 600 square miles, and is home to more than seven million people. Our city is one of the most creative and diverse in the world, containing the art, literature and history of all mankind. London has helped shape the world as we know it, inspiring figures such as Gandhi, Jimi Hendrix, Charles Darwin, Claude Monet and Karl Marx. Dr Johnson's words are more true now than ever.

However, sometimes we forget how lucky we are to be here. *Tired of London, Tired of Life* began because I felt I had become weary of living in London. I set myself a challenge to discover new things to do, and secretly began to form my own collection of London's hidden delights. As the list grew, I decided to offer it to others seeking inspiration, eventually making a New Year's resolution a few years ago to share a new idea every day online.

When I started to look around me, I found an almost infinite number of things to do in London: in one day in our capital city, you can experience the grey fog of an English morning, the heat of the tropics, the cold of the arctic and the humidity of the rainforest; you can meet someone from any country in the world; eat cuisine from six continents; and take a journey to the outer reaches of the solar system.

This book continues the project, showcasing some of the most interesting experiences that the city has to offer, matched by month and season to help you to make the most of our capital city.

Tom Jones – January 2012
www.tiredoflondontiredoflife.com

January

Notes

1 January

Watch the New Year's Day Parade

Since 1987, the streets of London have hosted a New Year's Day Parade, with up to 10,000 performers from around the world taking to the streets, watched by half a million spectators.

The modern parade brings together all of London's boroughs for a march that passes some of Central London's most iconic landmarks. It's a great way to blow away those New Year cobwebs and start January on a high.

www.londonparade.co.uk
Nearest tubes: Westminster, Piccadilly Circus

2 January

Admire General Wolfe's view

ON HIS BIRTHDAY

Gazing out from his plinth beside the Royal Observatory in Greenwich Park, the statue of local man General James Wolfe has one of the finest views in London.

Looking out over the Old Naval College and across to the towers of Canary Wharf, the statue was given by Canada in 1930 to recognise the General's command of victorious British forces at Quebec, where he was shot and fatally wounded.

www.royalparks.gov.uk
Nearest rail: Blackheath, Greenwich, Maze Hill

3 January

Eat at the World's first museum café

Deep within the corridors of the Victoria & Albert Museum, the Morris, Gamble and Poynter Refreshment Rooms are a great place to rest the legs after seeing an exhibition. They are an original part of the museum building, having opened in 1857 as the first museum restaurant in the world.

Decorated in a very grand Arts & Crafts style, they still house a café serving a range of different dishes and drinks. On weekends there is even a live pianist to entertain visitors.

www.vam.ac.uk
Address: Cromwell Road, South Kensington, SW7 2RL
Nearest tube: South Kensington

4 January

Climb to the top of St Paul's Cathedral

The breathtaking view from the top of St Paul's Cathedral's classical dome is one of London's finest, and is the crowning glory of the work of Sir Christopher Wren, whose designs shaped London after the Great Fire.

Legend has it the cathedral elders wanted a more traditional design, and Wren promised them just that, safe in the knowledge they'd be long dead by the time his masterpiece was completed.

www.stpauls.co.uk
Address: St Paul's Churchyard, EC4M 8AD

• •

5 January

Visit Middle Temple

ON TWELFTH NIGHT

Occupying some of the country's finest real estate between the Thames and Fleet Street, Middle Temple is an Inn of Court founded for trainee lawyers in the 14th century.

The centrepiece of the Temple is Middle Temple Hall, a beautiful Elizabethan Hall in which Shakespeare's *Twelfth Night* was first performed. Members of the public are free to wander the grounds at certain times, but sadly access to the hall is limited.

www.middletemple.org.uk
Address: Middle Temple Lane, EC4Y 9AT
Nearest tube: Temple

• •

6 January

Warm up in the Milkbar, Soho

Found on a busy street in Soho, Milkbar is a stylish little cafe specialising in teas, coffees and cakes, served in attractive surroundings and vintage teacups.

It's a haven from the hustle and bustle outside, especially on dark wintry days when the weather is grey and cold, and on popular days the windows begin to steam up, cutting off the happy customers inside from the world.

Address: 3 Bateman Street, Soho, W1D 4AG
Nearest tubes: Tottenham Court Road, Leicester Square

7 January

ATTEND THE LONDON BOAT SHOW

Every January since the 1950s, boatbuilders, enthusiasts and chandlers from around the world have gathered together in London for the London Boat Show.

In recent years, the show has attracted over 100,000 visitors, with hundreds of different boats on show.

www.londonboatshow.com
Address: ExCeL London, Royal Victoria Dock, E16 1XL
Nearest DLR: Custom House

• •

8 January

BUY A BOOK AT PRIMROSE HILL BOOKS

Primrose Hill Books is a small independent bookshop on the lively Regent's Park Road in North London.

Situated in a tidy Victorian terrace of independent shops, the owners pride themselves on their wide selection of books and knowledgeable staff.

www.primrosehillbooks.com
Address: Primrose Hill Books, 134 Regent's Park Road, NW1 8XL
Nearest tube: Chalk Farm

9 January

Take a walk in Kelsey Park

Kelsey Park, in Beckenham, was previously part of the estate of Kelsey Manor, and was not opened to the public until 1913.

While the original Gothic Manor House was demolished in the 1920s, some relics of its past remain, with a large ornamental lake rich in wildlife, where Mandarin ducks and herons can be seen in January.

www.fokp.org
Address: Entrances at Manor Way Entrance, Wickham Road and Stone Park Avenue, Beckenham
Nearest rail: Beckenham Junction

10 January

Drink in the Queen's Head at Downe

While red TfL buses stop outside the Queen's Head in the small Kentish village of Downe, and it is technically in London, the atmosphere is distinctly villagey. Perfect for a cosy winter drink.

The village where Charles Darwin lived has changed little over the years, and the pub dates back to 1565, when it was named in honour of Queen Elizabeth I, following her visit to the village.

www.queensheaddowne.co.uk
Address: 25 High Street Downe, Kent BR6 7US

11 January

Experience a London fog

Evelyn Waugh wrote of London that 'We designed a city which was meant to be seen in a fog', and although the deadly pea-soupers of Victorian London are a thing of the past, London is still at its most atmospheric on foggy days.

There is something particularly special about the fog which hangs low over the city on a cold day, obscuring well-known landmarks and giving the capital a mysterious air.

12 January

Explore the Palm House at Kew

Winter never comes to Kew's Palm House, which since 1848 has been home to exotic palms and plants collected from all around the world, recreating the conditions of a tropical rainforest.

The house is one of the world's most important surviving Victorian greenhouses, and visitors can climb up to the treetops and see the palms from above, while down in the darkened basement there is a marine display with live fish in tanks.

www.kew.org
Address: Kew, Richmond, Surrey TW9 3AB
Nearest tube: Kew Gardens

13 January

Embrace the past at the Reminiscence Centre

Blackheath's Age Exchange Reminiscence Centre was founded in 1983 as part of a project to recognise the value of the past and gather the memories of older members of the community.

The centre is home to a café where people of all ages gather, as well as a museum of everyday life, bringing together early-20th-century objects. It also provides opportunities for schoolchildren to meet with older people to help them learn about their past.

www.age-exchange.org.uk
Address: 11 Blackheath Village, SE3 9LA
Nearest rail: Blackheath

14 January

Drink in a bar made of Swedish ice

Sometimes an overcast and rainy January can be disappointing, so if you're after a full-blown Arctic experience, you need to go that extra mile.

The people at Ice Bar in Soho have cottoned on to this and built a permanent wintry experience out of ice harvested from the Torne River in Northern Sweden, and kept permanently at -5 degrees centigrade. The bar offers visitors the opportunity to experience an Arctic winter without ever leaving the capital.

www.belowzerolondon.com
Address: 31–33 Heddon Street, W1B 4BN
Nearest tubes: Oxford Circus, Piccadilly Circus

15 January

VISIT THE KEW BRIDGE STEAM MUSEUM

Originally built by the Victorians to supply London with water, today Kew Bridge Steam Museum is home to one of the best collections of rotative steam engines in the world.

The site is also home to the Waterworks Railway, a tiny two-foot gauge railway, which is London's only passenger-carrying steam railway.

www.kbsm.org
Address: Green Dragon Lane, Brentford, TW8 0EN
Nearest tube: Gunnersbury, Kew Gardens

Watch the flood forecasting lions

A line of fierce lions keeps watch along the Thames in Central London. The lions, which were designed by Timothy Butler and installed as part of Sir Joseph Bazalgette's Victorian sewage works programme, hold mooring rings in their mouths, but also act as a flood-warning system for superstitious Londoners, keen to keep an eye on water levels in the Thames.

It is said that:

'When the lions drink, London will sink
When it's up to their manes, we'll go down the drains
When the water is sucked, you can be sure we're all ... in trouble.'

So, if the level of the Thames reaches their mouths, there is a risk of London flooding.

17 January

Explore the Petrie Museum

The Petrie Museum of Egyptian Archaeology, which is found at the top of a windy staircase at University College, London, was established in 1892 as a teaching resource for UCL's Department of Egyptian Archaeology and Philology.

It houses an estimated 80,000 objects covering all aspects of life in the Nile Valley, all placed in dark and eerie cases, with visitors offered torches to navigate the corridors.

www.ucl.ac.uk/museums/petrie
Address: Malet Place, WC1E 6BT
Nearest tubes: Euston Square, Russell Square

18 January

Tour the Fuller's Brewery

Fuller's London Pride is a ubiquitous beer across the pubs of London, and at the Griffin Brewery in Chiswick, Fuller's have been brewing beer for over 150 years, though it is thought the site has been the home of brewing for two centuries longer.

While still very much a working brewery, Fuller's run around twenty tours a week, with guides talking visitors through the brewing process, and there are tasting sessions afterwards.

www.fullers.co.uk/rte.asp?id=9
Address: Chiswick Lane South, W4 2QB
Nearest tube: Turnham Green

19 January

Embrace feminism at The Women's Library

Established in 1926, the Women's Library in East London is a cultural centre and library which holds probably the most comprehensive collections of documents and books on women's history in the UK.

The Library hosts regular exhibitions and also has a reading room, which is free and open to all. In 2002, the library moved from a basement in London Guildhall University to its current location on the site of two former East End wash houses.

www.londonmet.ac.uk/thewomenslibrary/
Address: London Metropolitan University, 25 Old Castle Street, E1 7NT
Nearest tubes: Aldgate East, Aldgate

20 January

Have breakfast at Pellicci's

A classic café in every sense, E. Pellicci, on Bethnal Green Road, was Grade II-listed by English Heritage in 2005.

The café has been run by the Pellicci family since 1900, and combines a traditional East End atmosphere with a classic Italian café in a space created by carpenter Achille Capocciin in 1946.

www.classiccafes.co.uk/Pelliccifeature.htm
Address: 332 Bethnal Green Road, E2 0AG
Nearest tube: Bethnal Green

21 January

Visit the Florence Nightingale Museum

The Florence Nightingale Museum, on Lambeth Palace Road, is a museum celebrating the famous nurse, and exhibits a unique collection of artefacts from her life.

Nightingale's story is charted from her privileged birth, to her battles against social convention, and her historical status as one of the most famous and influential women of the 19th century.

www.florence-nightingale.co.uk
Address: 2 Lambeth Palace Road SE1 7EW
Nearest tubes: Westminster, Waterloo

22 January

Enjoy a drink at the Lord Clyde

The Lord Clyde, in Borough, is a perfect little pub, rebuilt in 1913 on a site that has served thirsty Londoners for over 300 years. The pub's exterior is notable for its red-brown English-bond brickwork and façade of glazed earthenware tiles.

The Lord Clyde was taken over by Denis and Molly Fitzpatrick in 1956, and has been run by the family for three generations (over fifty years).

www.lordclyde.com
Address: 27 Clennam Street, SE1 1ER
Nearest tube: Borough

• •

23 January

Contemplate in the Tibetan Peace Garden

Opened by the Dalai Lama in 1999, the Tibetan Peace Garden is a restful haven, found beside the Imperial War Museum in Lambeth.

The centrepiece of the garden is a traditional Tibetan-style Kalachakra Mandala, surrounded by modern sculptures, native Himalayan flowers and shrubs, and eight benches representing the eight elements of the noble eightfold path, a key part of Buddhist philosophy.

Address: Geraldine Mary Harmsworth Park, St George's Road, SE1 6ER
Nearest tubes: Elephant & Castle, Lambeth North

THINGS TO DO TODAY:

• •

24 January

Learn about the Foundling Hospital

The Foundling Museum, in Bloomsbury, was built in the 1930s, although it contains three rooms with interiors from the 18th century, and a staircase from the original Foundling Hospital in Lamb's Conduit Fields.

Through various displays, visitors are shown not only the history of the hospital and those who were raised in it, but also an amazing collection of art which was the first public collection in the country, as well as rooms noting the stories of three of the hospital's famous benefactors, Thomas Coram, William Hogarth and George Frideric Handel.

www.foundlingmuseum.org.uk
Address: 40 Brunswick Square, WC1N 1AZ
Nearest tubes: Russell Square, Kings Cross

25 January

ATTEND A BURNS NIGHT SCOTTISH DANCE

BURNS NIGHT

The London branch of the Royal Scottish Country Dance Society is more than eighty years old, and around Burns Night – which commemorates the life and work of Scotland's most famous poet, Robert Burns – it usually holds a programme of dances to celebrate the season.

During the rest of the year, the society runs classes for all abilities across the London area, while their prize-winning London branch demonstration team can also provide displays of Scottish dance.

www.rscdslondon.org.uk

26 January

BUY TEA AND CAKE AT THE GALLERY CAFÉ, BETHNAL GREEN

Bethnal Green's Gallery Café is a pleasant oasis beside the **York Hall Leisure Centre** and the **Bethnal Green Museum of Childhood**. It is run by **St Margarets House Settlement**, a charity devoted to providing space, opportunities and support to charities and community organisations in Tower Hamlets.

The cafe has plenty of tables, serves good vegetarian food and is home to a useful community noticeboard. They also have an alcohol licence and stage various events and regular music evenings.

www.stmargaretshouse.org.uk/gallery-cafe/gallery-cafe
Address: St Margaret's House, 21 Old Ford Road,
Bethnal Green, E2 9PL
Nearest tube: Bethnal Green

27 January

Shelter in the Turbine Hall at the Tate Modern

During the winter months, the Turbine Hall at the Tate Modern becomes a welcome haven for weary tourists, with plenty of room to escape the often challenging climate outdoors.

Home to power generation equipment until the mid-1990s, and adapted by Swiss architects Herzog & de Meuron, the Hall now offers a huge space which has been home to some of the capital's most talked-about art for over a decade, with commissions occupying the vast floorspace.

www.tate.org.uk/modern
Address: Bankside, SE1 9TG
Nearest tubes: Southwark, Mansion House, St Paul's

28 January

Take in the view from the Blue Bridge

The Blue Bridge, in St James's Park, is a lovely spot, with stunning views in both directions over the lake to Buckingham Palace, or Whitehall, Horse Guards, the Foreign and Commonwealth Office or the London Eye in the East.

It makes for a perfect pause on a wintry stroll, but don't stop too long or you might be confronted by the headless ghost of the wife of a sergeant, who was beheaded and thrown into the lake in the 1780s, and has been known to stalk the area after dark.

www.royalparks.gov.uk/St-Jamess-Park.aspx
Nearest tube: St James's Park

29 January

Visit the Fan Museum

The world's only museum dedicated purely to fans, The Fan Museum in Greenwich has been extolling the virtues of airflow devices from around the world for more than twenty years.

The museum opened in 1991 in a pair of Grade II-listed buildings constructed in 1721. Alongside the fan collection, there is also an Orangery overlooking a secret fan-shaped formal garden with a pond, stream and oriental architectural features.

www.fan-museum.org
Address: 12 Crooms Hill, Greenwich, SE10 8ER
Nearest rail: Greenwich

30 January

Have a drink in a galleried coaching inn

Owned and protected by the National Trust, and run by a private company, the George Inn in Southwark is London's only remaining galleried coaching inn, and dates from the 1670s.

Passengers once stayed here before setting off by stagecoach from ancient Watling Street for Canterbury; either as pilgrims, or heading for the sea ports beyond, bound for the continent.

Address: George Inn Yard, 77 Borough High Street, Southwark, SE1 1NH
Nearest tube: London Bridge

31 January

Catch the last tube

There's something very satisfying about catching the last tube home. After midnight, passengers still rarely speak to each other, but there is a faint glimmer of camaraderie which is not present the rest of the time. Having beaten the deadline, riders are whisked home towards their beds.

Catching the last tube is not a tourist experience, but there's something quintessentially London about it, especially in January when there are fewer people partying around town.

www.tfl.gov.uk

February

• •

1 February

TOUR HMS *BELFAST*

Moored a short walk from Tower Bridge is **HMS** *Belfast*, a large ship which saw active service in the Second World War. It famously served protecting the Arctic convoys to the Soviet Union, when chilly sailors kept watch for German U-boats from its decks.

In 1971, it was saved from destruction and towed to London to start a new life as a museum. Today its story is told through helpful guides, first-hand accounts of those who served on it, and a chance to go below decks to see the cabins and engine rooms to get a sense of what life was like aboard.

www.hmsbelfast.iwm.org.uk
Address: Morgan's Lane, Tooley Street, SE1 2JH
Nearest tubes: London Bridge, Tower Hill

2 February

Take a walk on the Thames foreshore

The Thames in Central London has a significant tidal range, and at low tide a large area of foreshore opens up to be explored; the area is littered with a range of ancient and modern items which can tell us a great deal about the river's history.

Ballast cast off from ancient ships is mixed with wooden piles from long-demolished piers, all smoothed by the ebb and flow of the river. The tides can be dangerous, so check with an expert before descending the steps to river level.

3 February

Go shopping at Liberty & Co

Liberty department store, designed by architects Edwin T. Hall and Edwin S. Hall in a mock-Tudor style, was constructed in 1924 using original timbers from the HMS *Impregnable* and HMS *Hindustan*.

The resulting iconic store is recognised as one of the finest buildings of the Tudor revival Arts and Crafts movement, and is home to an interesting store selling a range of clothes, gifts and furniture.

www.liberty.co.uk
Address: Great Marlborough Street, W1B 5AH
Nearest tubes: Oxford Circus, Piccadilly Circus

4 February

Meet the dinosaurs at the Natural History Museum

The striking dinosaur skeletons are one of the most memorable parts of any visit to the Natural History Museum.

Alongside the huge Diplodocus cast, which greets visitors in the huge main hall, is a Triceratops, a half-buried Edmontosaurus and a terrifying T. Rex.

www.nhm.ac.uk
Address: Cromwell Road, SW7 5BD
Nearest tubes: South Kensington, Gloucester Road

5 February

ADMIRE THE BRUTALISM OF TRELLICK TOWER

Set against the grey February skies, Brutalist Trellick Tower is at its most bleak. Designed by the architect Ernest Goldfinger, it was completed in 1972 and awarded Grade II*-listed status in the late 1990s.

Brutalism apparently derived its name from the French *béton brut*, meaning 'raw concrete', which is a fine description of the Trellick. The Tower contains 217 flats and is characterised by a separate lift shaft, linked at every third floor to the main building.

Address: Golborne Road, London W10 5PL
Nearest tube: Westbourne Park

6 February

Shop at Kiwi Fruits

ON WAITANGI DAY

London has a significant population of New Zealanders, who come together on Waitangi Day to remember their motherland. Many of them are aided by some home comforts from Kiwi Fruits, a shop beneath New Zealand House which has been importing goods for homesick Kiwis since 1983.

Most of their offerings are imported directly from New Zealand, with books, food, native wood crafts and even traditional bone and pounamu carvings.

www.kiwifruitsnzshop.com
Address: 7 Royal Opera Arcade, SW1Y 4UY
Nearest tube: Piccadilly Circus

7 February

See the snowdrops in Petts Wood

A piece of the country in South-East London, Petts Wood covers more than 300 acres, and is owned and managed by the National Trust. In February, the first of the snowdrops begin to push up from the woodland floor, as a symbol that winter will soon be over.

Petts Wood is made up of a variety of oak, ash, birch, hornbeam and sweet chestnut trees, and contains land formerly part of the Hawkwood Estate and Edlmann Wood.

www.nationaltrust.org.uk
Nearest rail: Petts Wood, Chislehurst

8 February

Visit the barge graveyard at Rainham

Derelict barges litter the banks of the Thames beside Ferry Lane in Rainham, built to support the floating piers of the Mulberry harbours used during the D-Day landings in Normandy.

Today, they offer an interesting insight into Britain's wartime past, and the area has spectacular views across the river to industrial South-East London.

Nearest rail: Rainham

9 February

Discover the World Time Today clock

Amongst the crowds in Piccadilly Circus tube station, take a moment to stop and view the World Time Today clock. The clock was added by architect Charles Holden and builder John Mowlem & Co when they refurbished the station between 1925 and 1928.

The clock's time band moves across its central line at the same pace as the earth rotates, and shows the rough time at any point on the map.

Tube: Piccadilly Circus

THINGS TO DO TODAY:

10 February

DRINK IN THE PUB WHERE LENIN AND STALIN 'FIRST MET'

While recorded history dictates that Joseph Stalin first met Vladimir Ilyich Lenin at the Bolshevik Congress in Tsarist Finland in 1905, some claim that they actually met a couple of years earlier in the pub which is now called the Crown Tavern, on Clerkenwell Green.

Lenin had recently moved the publication of the Russian socialist newspaper *Iskra* to Clerkenwell Green, and was living on nearby Percy Circus, a short walk away. Legend has it that they met in the pub when Stalin came to London to train as a Bolshevik.

11 February

Search out the Mandela Way Tank

Since the 1990s, a T-34 tank has occupied a prime spot between Mandela Way and Page's Walk, in South London. Built for the Russian army, it was probably used in Czechoslovakia in the Prague Spring of 1968.

The tank was imported for use in films, before being passed to a property developer, who installed it in its current spot.

Address: Mandela Way, SE1
Nearest tube: Elephant and Castle

12 February

Go skating at the Lee Valley Ice Centre

Opened in January 1984 by Olympic gold medallists Jayne Torvill and Christopher Dean, the Lee Valley Ice Centre is an internationally sized ice rink, which can host over a thousand skaters and spectators.

The centre is home to the Lee Valley Lions ice-hockey team, as well as four synchronised skating teams, and there are also public skating sessions every day.

www.leevalleypark.org.uk
Address: Lea Bridge Road, Leyton, E10 7QL
Nearest tubes: Walthamstow Central, Leyton

13 February

Explore the Bevis Marks Synagogue

The oldest synagogue in Britain still in use, the Bevis Marks Synagogue was completed in 1701 and awarded Grade I-listed status in 1950. Today, the synagogue has a thriving congregation and plays an important role for Jewish people working in the City of London.

It was here that the writer Isaac D'Israeli, father of Prime Minister Benjamin Disraeli, worshipped until he left the congregation over a disputed fine, leading to Benjamin being baptised into the Church of England.

www.bevismarks.org.uk
Address: Bevis Marks, EC3
Nearest tubes: Liverpool Street, Aldgate

14 February

Seek out Aphrodite

ON ST VALENTINE'S DAY

At the heart of the Ancient Greece and Rome section of the British Museum is a romantic vision of Aphrodite, goddess of love, showing her crouching at her bath.

It is a version of a second-century statue, which echoes many similar statues that came out of the cult of Aphrodite.

www.britishmuseum.org
Address: Great Russell Street, WC1B 3DG
Nearest tubes: Holborn, Russell Square, Goodge Street

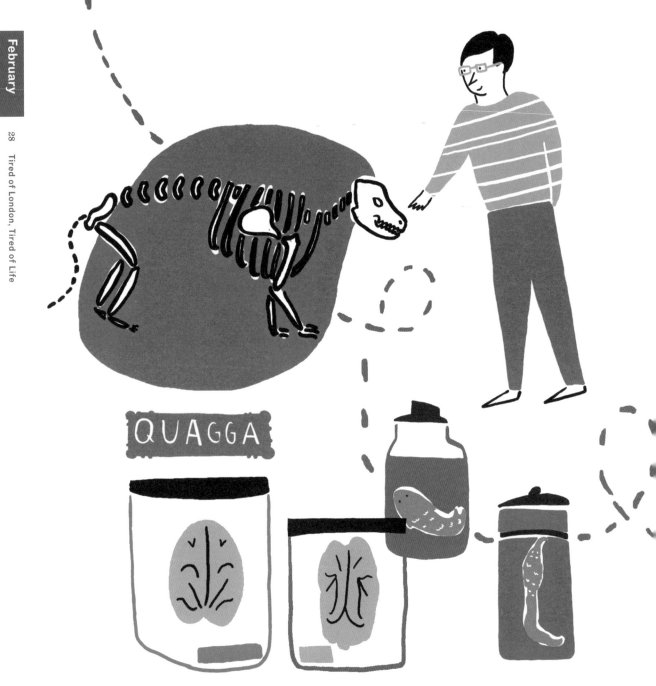

QUAGGA

15 February

Visit the Grant Museum of Zoology

Now housed in an atmospheric galleried hall in University College London's Rockefeller Building, the Grant Museum of Zoology is one of the oldest natural history collections in the country.

Founded in 1828, it is a testament to the British collectors of the Victorian age, and holds a range of interesting and rare animal skeletons and specimens, including a Tasmanian tiger, a quagga, and a dodo.

www.ucl.ac.uk/museums/zoology
Address: Rockefeller Building, University College London, 21 University Street, WC1E 6DE
Nearest tubes: Euston Square, Russell Square

DODO

16 February

Buy wine at Berry Bros and Rudd

Established in 1698 by the Widow Bourne, Berry Bros and Rudd has been trading wine from the same location opposite St James's Palace for more than three centuries.

Still owned and run by the Berry and Rudd families whose name it bears, past customers have included Lord Byron, William Pitt, George III and the Aga Khan, and today the store sells wine to both the Queen and the Prince of Wales.

www.bbr.com
Address: 3 St James's Street, SW1A 1EG
Nearest tube: Green Park

17 February

Drink at The Seven Stars

Notable for being one of only a few buildings in the area which date from before the Great Fire of 1666, the Seven Stars is right behind the Royal Courts of Justice and has understandably long been popular with the legal fraternity.

Today, the Seven Stars is run by chef Roxy Beaujolais, with the help of her cat Thomas Paine, which can often be seen running around wearing a Tudor ruff.

Address: Great Russell Street, WC1B 3DG
Nearest tubes: Holborn, Temple, Chancery Lane

18 February

Seek out the grave of Giro the dog

In the shadow of the Duke of York Column, at the top of the steps by the Royal Society and Carlton House Terrace, is the grave of Giro the Alsatian, whose owner Dr Leopold von Hoesch was a well-respected diplomat under both the Weimar Republic and Nazi Governments, and famously received a full Nazi funeral in London in 1936.

Giro died two years earlier, after chewing through an electrical wire and getting electrocuted. Being a dog, Giro had no idea what was going on in his home country. However, he is often judged guilty by association to the newly elected Nazi Government, and today is almost as famous as his late owner.

Address: 9 Carlton House Terrace, SW1Y 5AG
Nearest tube: Piccadilly Circus

19 February

See the Lord Mayor's Coach

On permanent display in the Museum of London, the Lord Mayor's Coach was designed by Sir Robert Taylor and built by Joseph Berry of Leather Lane, Holborn, in 1757.

The Coach is still used every year for the Lord Mayor's Parade, and over the years has been restored many times to ensure it can continue its service. Experts estimate that there are almost a hundred layers of paint and varnish on the ceiling of the coach.

www.museumoflondon.org.uk
Address: London Wall, EC2Y 5HN
Nearest tubes: Barbican, St Paul's, Moorgate

20 February

Meet the animals at the Clore Rainforest Lookout

On wintry days in Central London, it is easy to forget that there is a rainforest only a short distance away, with monkeys, lemurs and pygmy marmosets roaming right in the middle of London.

Opened in 2007 at London Zoo, the Clore Rainforest Lookout allows visitors to get up into the rainforest canopy, face to face with jungle animals.

www.zsl.org/zsl-london-zoo/exhibits/clore-rainforest-lookout
Address: ZSL London Zoo, Regent's Park, NW1 4RY
Nearest tubes: Camden Town, Regent's Park

21 February

Search the archives at Rotherhithe Picture Research Library

The Rotherhithe Picture Research Library is an educational charity, opened in 1976 as part of Sands Studios, and holds thousands of old photographs, postcards and magazines.

Pictures are classified by themes, countries and historical periods, to enable researchers to find what they are looking for, and the library is open to the public every weekday from 10 am until 4 pm.

www.sandsfilms.co.uk
Address: Sands Films Studio, 82 Saint Marychurch Street, SE16 4HZ
Nearest tube: Rotherhithe

22 February

Drink at the Fitzroy Tavern

The Fitzroy Tavern, in Fitzrovia, was opened in 1883 as the Fitzroy Coffee House, and converted into a pub in 1887, by William Mortimer Brutton. However, it wasn't until the early years of the 20th century that it was acquired by Judah Morris Kleinfeld and given its current name, taken from the aristocratic Fitzroy family, who owned the whole area.

Between the 1920s and 1950s, the pub was a centre of literary and artistic London, and a favourite drinking haunt of the likes of Dylan Thomas, Augustus John and George Orwell.

Address: 16 Charlotte Street, Fitzrovia, W1T 2NA
Nearest tube: Goodge Street, Tottenham Court Road, Oxford Circus

• •

23 February

DRINK IN THE PUB WHERE PEPYS WATCHED LONDON BURN

ON HIS BIRTHDAY

Samuel Pepys is probably best known for his account of the Great Fire of London, and as it raged he escaped by boat and described in his diary how he took refuge in 'a little alehouse on bankside ... and there watched the fire grow'.

The Anchor still stands on the site of that alehouse, offering fantastic views towards the City, and Pepys was not the only famous Londoner to have visited, as Samuel Johnson was lent a room inside by the owners Henry and Hestor Thrale when formulating his dictionary.

24 February

Cross Paddington Basin's Rolling Bridge

Designed by the Thomas Heatherwick Studio, and installed in 2004, Paddington Basin's Rolling Bridge is an innovative approach to crossing the canal inlet.

When operated, the 12-metre Rolling Bridge slowly and smoothly curls unaided into a small octagon resembling a hamster's wheel, allowing craft to navigate the canal before rolling back out into its straight bridge form.

Notes

....

....

....

....

....

....

....

....

....

....

25 February

Take a joyride from Stapleford Airport

Tiny Stapleford Airport, a few miles from Epping Forest in Essex, opened in 1933, offering a scheduled service to Paris in a tiny Dragon Rapide. It later became a base for the fearsome 46 Squadron during the Second World War, before relaxing into semi-retirement as the home to the Herts and Essex, Stapleford Flying Club, who still operate it today.

The airport conducts regular sightseeing flights over Central London, offering a bird's eye view of landmarks such as the Millennium Dome, Tower Bridge, the Houses of Parliament, Trafalgar Square and Buckingham Palace.

www.flyingpresents.co.uk
Address: Stapleford Flight Centre Ltd, Essex RM4 1SJ

26 February

Listen for Wren's footsteps

Sir Christopher Wren once resided at the Old Court House, which faces on to Hampton Court Green, beside the River Thames, having leased the property from Queen Anne in lieu of unpaid fees.

Now a private house, it is marked by a plaque, and it is said his ghostly footsteps can often be heard nearby on the anniversary of his death.

Address: Old Court House, Hampton Court Green, East Molesey Richmond Upon Thames
Nearest rail: Hampton Court

28 February

Stock up at Algerian Coffee Stores

Opened in 1887, Algerian Coffee Stores, on Old Compton Street, stocks more than 80 coffees and 120 teas from around the world.

Inside and outside, the shop retains many of its original features, with shelves packed with coffee and a range of coffee paraphernalia, as well as fresh coffee sold over the counter to take away.

www.algcoffee.co.uk
Address: 52 Old Compton Street, W1D 4PB
Nearest tubes: Piccadilly Circus, Leicester Square

29 February

Explore Sigmund Freud's study

As war loomed large in Western Europe in the 1930s, Sigmund Freud escaped his native Austria and settled with his family on a leafy street in South Hampstead.

Although he died only a year later, his final home is preserved as a museum to his life and work, and his study is a fascinating place to visit, containing antiquities he collected from around the world, and – most importantly – the legendary psychoanalytic couch on which his patients reclined.

www.freud.org.uk
Address: 20 Maresfield Gardens, NW3 5SX
Nearest tube: Finchley Road

27 February

Browse the Southbank Centre Book Market

Echoing the bookstalls on Paris's Rive Gauche, the Southbank Centre Book Market, beneath Waterloo Bridge, is one of the only outdoor second-hand and antique book markets in London.

Thanks to the covering of the bridge, it is open every day until around 7 pm, whatever the weather, and, while the books are a little more expensive than at your local jumble sale, it's a lovely spot to search for something special.

Address: Queen's Walk, SE1
Nearest tube: Waterloo

March

1 March

See the daffodils in St James's Park

ON ST DAVID'S DAY

One clear sign that spring is on its way is the carpet of daffodils that begin to arrive amongst the trees in St James's Park.

Professional gardeners ensure that the park's blooms are at their best all year round, but it is at this time of year that the springtime eruption of daffodils suddenly captures the imagination.

www.royalparks.gov.uk/St-Jamess-Park.aspx
Nearest tube: St James's Park

2 March

Meet the animals on Woodlands Farm

One of the largest city farms in London, Woodlands Farm covers 89 acres, and is situated on the borders of Greenwich and Bexley boroughs in South-East London.

Originally a private working farm on woodland cleared in the 1790s, the site was threatened by plans to build a motorway, and it was only in 1997 that it passed to the Woodlands Farm Trust.

Today, it is home to sheep, cows, pigs and horses, as well as other farmyard animals, and it operates as a recreational and educational resource for local people of all ages.

www.thewoodlandsfarmtrust.org
Address: 331 Shooters Hill, Welling, Kent DA16 3RP
Nearest rail: Welling

3 March

VISIT THE FLOATING CAFÉ AT LITTLE VENICE

The Waterside Café in Little Venice is a pleasant little eatery situated on a barge in the canal.

The café offers teas and coffee to passers-by who can enjoy their refreshment on board, or spread out on the towpath to catch some rays of sunshine.

Address: Little Venice, Warwick Crescent, W2 6NE
Nearest tubes: Paddington, Warwick Avenue

....

....

....

....

....

....

....

4 March

See the 'Unlucky Mummy' at the British Museum

Probably the most popular rooms in the British Museum, rooms 62 and 63 are largely dedicated to death rituals of Ancient Egypt, and contain various coffins, mummies and funerary masks.

One of the most famous items is number 22542, the 'unlucky mummy' from the tomb of an unknown priestess who died in 950BC. Legend has it that the four Victorian travellers who first acquired it died mysteriously, and the man who delivered it to the Museum died within a week. When a photographer committed suicide after taking its picture, its reputation was sealed. It has even been blamed for the sinking of the *Titanic*.

www.britishmuseum.org
Address: Great Russell Street, WC1B 3DG
Nearest tubes: Holborn, Russell Square, Goodge Street

5 March

Drink at The Cove, London's Cornish theme pub

ON ST PIRAN'S DAY

Overlooking the plaza in front of St Paul's, Covent Garden, is The Cove, a small but welcoming Cornish theme pub, which is a great place to toast St Piran, the patron saint of Cornwall.

Accessed via a barely marked stairway in the Cornish pasty shop below, it offers Cornish ales and pasties brought up by dumb-waiter.

Address: 1 The Piazza, Covent Garden, WC2E 8HB
Nearest tube: Covent Garden, Leicester Square

6 March

Go shopping in Britain's first shopping arcade

Opened in 1819, Mayfair's Burlington Arcade was Britain's very first shopping arcade, built by Lord George Cavendish following years of frustration at passers-by throwing oyster shells into his garden.

The Arcade is notable for being patrolled by uniformed Burlington Arcade Beadles who wear top hats and tailcoats, and are charged with enforcing rules which prohibit whistling, carrying of large parcels, playing of musical instruments and running, amongst other heinous crimes.

www.burlington-arcade.co.uk
Address: Mayfair, W1
Nearest tubes: Piccadilly Circus, Green Park

7 March
Visit Electric Avenue

In the heart of multicultural Brixton, Electric Avenue was the first shopping street to be lit by electricity, and was the grand focal point of the area following its completion in 1888.

Today, the street made famous by Eddy Grant in his 1983 hit single is home to various shops reflecting the area's Caribbean, African, Arab and Portuguese communities, and also hosts a regular street market.

Nearest tube: Brixton

8 March

WALK THE PARKLAND WALK

The Northern Heights Parkland Walk is a four-and-a-half-mile walk along the former route of the London and North Eastern Railway between Finsbury Park and Alexandra Palace. The path takes walkers through Stroud Green, Crouch Hill, Highgate and Muswell Hill, passing various 'ghost' stations along the route.

Due to the linear nature of the former railway line, the walk is known as London's longest Local Nature Reserve, and it is a haven for plants and wildlife, including oak, ash, rowan, sycamore and yew trees, as well as butterflies, hedgehogs, slow-worms, and even muntjac deer.

9 March

Take tea at Fortnum & Mason

Afternoon tea at Fortnum & Mason, the department store established in 1707 by William Fortnum and Hugh Mason at 181 Piccadilly, is an institution.

Known by its reputation as the Queen's grocer, the store has a number of restaurants, including St James's Restaurant, on the fourth floor, which is one of London's most famous spots for tea, often accompanied by a live pianist.

www.fortnumandmason.com
Address: 181 Piccadilly, W1A 1ER
Nearest tubes: Piccadilly Circus, Green Park

10 March

Wander in Morden Hall Park

Situated beside the River Wandle in South London, Morden Hall Park is part of the Morden Estate, and was previously home to a tobacco mill.

In 1941, 125 acres of the estate were given to the National Trust, and the parkland is now open to visitors, who are also free to wander amongst many of the historic estate buildings.

www.nationaltrust.org.uk/main/w-mordenhallpark-2
Nearest tube: Morden

11 March

Visit the Brunel Museum

The Brunel Museum is located in an old engine house in Rotherhithe, and was once part of the famous tunnel of Sir Marc Isambard Brunel, which still carries trains beneath the Thames.

A relatively small museum, the Brunel charts the history of both Sir Marc Isambard Brunel and his railway pioneer son, Isambard Kingdom Brunel, with a particular focus on the tunnel itself.

www.brunel-museum.org.uk
Address: Railway Avenue, Rotherhithe, SE16 4LF
Nearest rail: Rotherhithe

12 March

See a film at the Coronet

Notting Hill's Coronet Cinema first opened in 1898 as a theatre, before diversifying into showing films, before becoming a full-time cinema in 1923.

After narrowly escaping plans to turn it into a fast-food restaurant in the late 1980s, the building was Grade II-listed, and went on to be a film star in its own right, with Hugh Grant and Julia Roberts visiting the cinema in the film *Notting Hill*.

www.coronet.org
Address: 103 Notting Hill Gate, W11 3LB
Nearest tube: Notting Hill Gate

13 March

Take in the view from the View Tube

Perched on the Greenway in East London, the View Tube is a café and community venue built from bright green recycled shipping containers.

The café opened in 2010, and is a lovely spot for a cup of tea, offering unrivalled views of the Olympic Park.

www.theviewtube.co.uk
Address: The Greenway, Marshgate Lane, E15 2PJ
Nearest DLR: Pudding Mill Lane

14 March

Examine the Dalston Peace Mural

Designed by Ray Walker and painted by Mike Jones and Anna Walker, the Dalston Peace Mural depicts the 1983 Dalston Peace Carnival, although the artists have allowed themselves some artistic licence in their creation.

The mural was funded by the GLC and Hackney Council, and unveiled in 1984 by Tony Banks MP, who was instrumental in approving funding. While Banks is no longer with us, the mural is still as vibrant as ever, and can be easily spotted by anyone wandering along Dalston Lane.

Address: Dalston, E8 3BG
Nearest tube: Dalston Junction

15 March

Step inside a 19th-century operating theatre

The Old Operating Theatre Museum is an original 19th-century operating theatre, purpose-built in 1822 in the roof of St Thomas's Church, Southwark, and it was formerly part of St Thomas's Hospital. The theatre was built in the church's herb garret, a space used by St Thomas's Apothecary to store and cure herbs.

In 1862, on Florence Nightingale's advice, the hospital began the move to its present site at Lambeth and the operating theatre was closed down and effectively boarded up in the roof space. There it remained hidden until rediscovered in an attic by Raymond Russell in 1956.

www.thegarret.org.uk
Address: 9a St Thomas Street, SE1 9RY
Nearest tube: London Bridge

16 March

Eat at the Hummingbird Bakery

Originally opened in 2004 on Portobello Road to provide Londoners with alternative cakes, the Hummingbird Bakery has grown into a baking sensation, with shops in South Kensington, Soho and Spitalfields.

Featuring signature bright cupcakes, the Hummingbird makes a point of making cakes on site at each branch, with fresh cakes each day and throughout the day.

www.hummingbirdbakery.com
Addresses: Old Brompton Road, Portobello Road, Wardour Street, Frying Pan Alley

17 March

Visit London's first Irish pub

ON ST PATRICK'S DAY

The Tipperary, at 66 Fleet Street, is London's oldest Irish pub. While the pub itself dates back as far as 1605, it only became an Irish pub around 1700, and was possibly the first pub outside Ireland to serve draught Guinness.

Originally called 'The Boar's Head', it was renamed The Tipperary after the First World War, in a nod to the song 'It's a long way to Tipperary', which many regulars had sung in the trenches.

Address: 66 Fleet Street, EC4Y 1HT
Nearest tubes: Temple, Chancery Lane

BORROW BOOKS FROM WESTMINSTER CHINESE LIBRARY

Serving the people of Chinatown with reading material which is often hard to access, the Westminster Chinese Library, in Charing Cross, is the country's largest Chinese language collection in a public library.

A team of four Chinese-speaking staff serve thousands of Chinese-speaking people from far and wide who come to use the library, which offers around 50,000 Chinese-language books for loan and reference, as well as music cassettes, CDs, and videos.

www3.westminster.gov.uk/libraries/chinese
Address: Charing Cross Library, Charing Cross Road, WC2H 0HF
Nearest tubes: Leicester Square, Charing Cross

19 March

Touch a meteorite

The Planetarium in Greenwich houses part of the Gideon Meteorite, a 4.5bn year old piece of iron and nickel which was found in the Namibian Desert.

The £16 million Planetarium opened at the Royal Observatory at Greenwich in 2007, and houses interactive displays about the universe, including the meteorite.

www.nmm.ac.uk/places/royal-observatory/planetarium
Address: Royal Observatory, Blackheath Ave, SE10 8XJ
Nearest rail: Blackheath, Greenwich

20 March

Sit beside the Roman London Wall

There are a number of places in London where you can see London Wall, but tiny St Alphage Gardens, beside the Barbican Centre, offers a chance to see the Wall up close, and even touch it.

The former churchyard of St Alphage church, the garden was opened to the public in 1872, and the old Roman Wall can be found inside.

Address: London Wall, EC2
Nearest tubes: Moorgate, Liverpool Street

21 March

Drink wine at El Vino

Serving the City of London for more than 125 years, El Vino was established as Bower and Co in 1879 by Alfred Bower, a rare unlicensed 'Free Vintner'. Bower decided to cease trading under his own name when he became Lord Mayor of London, and changed the name to El Vino in 1923.

Today, the company operates various wine bars, but one of the oldest is the flagship Fleet Street bar, which was built in a converted hall of mirrors.

www.elvino.co.uk
Address: 47 Fleet Street, EC4Y 1BJ
Nearest tube: Chancery Lane

22 March

Visit Hackney's oldest house

A Grade II*-listed house on Homerton High Street, Sutton House was built in 1535 by Sir Ralph Sadleir, a courtier of Henry VIII. It was acquired by the National Trust in the 1930s and used as a fire warden centre until the 1980s, before opening to the public in 1991.

Alongside the house and museum, there is also an excellent tea room, an art gallery and gift shop, as well as some well-stocked shelves of second-hand books for sale, an art gallery and gift shop.

www.nationaltrust.org.uk/main/w-suttonhouse
Address: 2 and 4 Homerton High Street, Hackney, E9 6JQ
Nearest rail: Hackney Central

23 March

Drink at Ye Olde Cheshire Cheese

Up an alleyway off Fleet Street, Ye Olde Cheshire Cheese is one of London's most celebrated pubs, known to have been visited by Mark Twain and Alfred Tennyson. The pub was referred to in Charles Dickens' *A Tale of Two Cities*, and he is said to have spent hours in his favourite seat to the right of the fireplace in the ground-floor bar.

The pub was one of the first to be rebuilt after the Great Fire of London, and what it lacks in natural light, it makes up for in atmosphere, with sawdust on the floor and features listed in the National Inventory of Historic Pub Interiors.

Address: 145 Fleet Street, EC4A 2BU
Nearest tube: Chancery Lane

24 March

Find the ultimate blue plaque

One of the most celebrated blue plaques in London is for someone perhaps not everyone has heard of, for at 16 Eaton Place, Belgravia, is a plaque commemorating William Ewart MP, the father of the blue plaque system.

Ewart lived here from 1830 until 1838, and was a notable reformer who, as well as being the first to propose a scheme for commemorating famous homes, was responsible for the Act that introduced public libraries.

Address: 16 Eaton Place, Belgravia, SW1X
Nearest tubes: Hyde Park Corner, Sloane Square

25 March

Take a trip on Hammerton's Ferry

Running daily between Orleans Road in Twickenham and Ham House in Richmond, from March until October, Hammerton's Ferry was established in 1909 by local man Walter Hammerton.

It is still running today, offering walkers and cyclists a useful way to cross the river, for a small fee. While the current ferry uses a modern speedboat, Hammerton's original skiff is still on display in the Museum of Docklands.

www.hammertonsferry.co.uk
Address: Orleans Road, Twickenham, Middlesex TW1 3BL

● ●

26 March

Buy fresh from Bangladesh at Taj Stores

ON THE NATIONAL DAY OF BANGLADESH

Brick Lane is the centre of London's Bengali community, and Taj Stores is a fantastic supermarket which was founded in 1936, and has served the local community with seasonal produce ever since.

Those worried about food miles should probably avoid produce flown daily from Bangladesh, but some of the unusual offerings in the store make it well worth a visit, with a wide selection of fresh exotic fruits and vegetables, as well as halal meats, and fish fresh from the Bay of Bengal.

www.tajstores.co.uk
Address: 112 Brick Lane, Spitalfields, E1 6RL
Nearest tube: Liverpool Street, Aldgate East

27 March

Search for paperbacks at the Broadway Bookshop

A fantastic little independent bookshop on Broadway Market, the Broadway Bookshop is small, but tucks books away into every nook and cranny, so there's plenty on offer.

The shop has a loyal customer base which ensures a good turnover of books, and it also hosts regular events with local and national authors, allowing them to showcase their wares. It is also a great place to stock up on Hackney news, via the busy noticeboard and gossip at the counter.

www.broadwaybookshophackney.com
Address: 6 Broadway Market, Hackney, E8 4QJ
Nearest tube: Bethnal Green

28 March

Climb the Wellington Arch

The Wellington Arch, on Hyde Park Corner, was built to commemorate Britain's victories in the Napoleonic Wars, and was planned to line up with Marble Arch and form a grand entrance into London from the west.

Today, surrounded by traffic, the Arch echoes Paris's Arc De Triomphe, with three floors of exhibits inside detailing its history, including the time it spent as London's smallest police station. There is also a viewing gallery offering a chance to peek into the gardens at Buckingham Palace and see who is on the tennis courts.

www.english-heritage.org.uk/daysout/properties/wellington-arch
Address: Apsley Way, Hyde Park Corner, W1J 7JZ
Nearest tube: Hyde Park Corner

29 March

Go to the top of Westminster Cathedral tower

Westminster Cathedral is the largest Roman Catholic church in England, and the centre of the Catholic Church, also acting as the seat of the Catholic Archbishop of Westminster.

The Cathedral was designed by Victorian architect John Francis Bentley to reflect the Byzantine style of early Christianity, and the first stone was laid in 1895. It is topped off by a 273 ft tower, dedicated to St Edward the Confessor, with a public viewing gallery at the top, offering views out across Central London.

www.westminstercathedral.org.uk
Address: Cathedral Clergy House, 42 Francis Street, SW1P 1QW
Nearest tube: Victoria

Notes

....

....

....

....

....

....

....

....

30 March

Visit the Holland Park Kyoto Garden

The Holland Park Kyoto Garden was created in 1991 by a team sponsored by the Kyoto Chamber of Commerce.

Refurbished in 2001, the gardens are laid out in a traditional Japanese style and are designed to commemorate the centenary of Britain's friendship with Japan, diplomatically overlooking the fact that the surrounding gardens and woodland only came into public ownership after Holland House was bombed during a war in which the countries were on opposite sides.

www.rbkc.gov.uk
Address: Ilchester Place, W8
Nearest tubes: Holland Park, Kensington High Street or Notting Hill!

31 March

Walk among the ruins of Lesnes Abbey

In parkland below Abbey Wood in South-East London are the ruins of Lesnes Abbey, founded by Richard de Luci in 1178. Only the ruined walls and a small visitors centre remain today, but this was once a grand abbey.

The Abbey was finally dissolved by Henry VIII, and the buildings fell into disrepair. Only in the 20th century was the site once again recognised as historically significant, and land ownership passed to London County Council around 1930.

www.bexley.gov.uk/index.aspx?articleid=3906
Nearest rail: Abbey Wood

April

SEEK OUT THE GRAVES OF FOOLS

ON APRIL FOOLS DAY

In Tudor times, the court jester played a key role in the Royal Household, acting as head fool, entertaining members of the court and – some academics believe – helping to defuse court tensions by delivering bad or embarrassing news to royalty.

Two of history's most famous fools are thought to be buried in unmarked graves at St Leonard's Church, in Shoreditch, where church records mark the deaths of William Somers, jester to Henry VIII and Richard Tarlton, Elizabeth I's favourite jester and the reputed inspiration for the character of Bottom in Shakespeare's *A Midsummer Night's Dream.*

Address: Shoreditch High Street, City of London E1 6JN
Nearest tube: Old Street

2 April

Visit Europe's first Thai Temple

The Buddhapadipa Temple, in Wimbledon, was the first Thai temple ever built in Europe. The temple originated in Richmond in 1965 and moved to its current location in Wimbledon, in 1976.

The temple has become an important European Buddhist training centre, and its grounds are grounds are open to visitors as long as they observe the rules. They cover approximately four acres and include an ornamental lake, a small grove, a flower garden and an orchard.

www.buddhapadipa.org
Address: 14 Calonne Road, Wimbledon, SW19 5HJ
Nearest tube: Wimbledon Park

3 April

Explore model London

The centrepiece of Bloomsbury's New London Architecture galleries is the Pipers Central London Model, a model of Central London built to a scale of 1:1500.

At 12 × 5 metres, it shows Central London between the Royal Docks in Docklands and Paddington, Battersea and King's Cross. The rest of the centre also houses a range of changing exhibitions covering subjects such as London's history, energy, water, environment, hotels and retail. These change throughout the year to keep the centre fresh.

www.newlondonarchitecture.org
Address: The Building Centre, 26 Store Street, WC1E 7BT
Nearest tube: Goodge Street, Tottenham Court Road

Browse for umbrellas at James Smith and Sons

Fine solutions to April showers have been offered by James Smith and Sons Umbrellas Ltd since the company's foundation in 1830.

The company still manufactures walking sticks and umbrellas in its basement workshops, and is an unrivalled destination for any brolliologist.

www.james-smith.co.uk
Address: Hazelwood House, 53 New Oxford Street, London WC1A 1BL
Nearest tube: Tottenham Court Road

5 April

Drink in a Victorian Gin Palace

The Princess Louise, in Holborn, is a Grade II-listed pub owned by the Samuel Smiths brewery. It was built in 1872 and is named after Queen Victoria's fourth daughter, Princess Louise.

One of the finest remaining examples of a Victorian Gin Palace, the pub has a fantastic interior dating from the 19th century with tiling by W.B. Simpson of Clapham, and is also notable for its Victorian lavatories.

Address: 208–209 High Holborn, WC1V 7BW
Nearest tube: Holborn, Covent Garden

6 April

Walk the Barbican High Walks

The Barbican Estate is a marvel of modernist architecture, and is an excellent place for a walk if the weather is getting you down. Architects Chamberlin, Powell and Bon included a network of covered walkways in their design – influenced by French architecture of the period – to create an urban village where not only are pedestrians separated from the streets below, they are also sheltered from the weather above.

While the walkways are a bit of a maze, getting lost is half the fun and there is always a map on hand to direct the uninitiated to the nearest tube station, museum, arts centre, greenhouse, church or school, all of which are found within the estate.

Nearest tube: Barbican

7 April

Find Bleeding Heart Yard

Given its name, it's no surprise that Clerkenwell's Bleeding Heart Yard has a gruesome story. Legend has it that Lady Hatton sold her soul to the devil and eventually a hooded figure showed up to her Annual Winter Ball to call in the debt.

She was led out of the room to a sudden clap of lightning, followed by a piercing scream. Her body was later found, torn limb from limb, with her heart pumping blood out into the yard.

Address: Bleeding Heart Yard, off Greville Street, EC1N 8SJ
Nearest tube: Farringdon

8 April

See the Tower Hill Memorial

Twin memorials at Tower Hill commemorate members of the Merchant Navy and fishing fleets who died during the First and Second World Wars. The grand colonnade, designed by Edwin Lutyens, was dedicated to those who died in the Great War, and was joined in 1955 by a semi-circular sunken garden dedicated to commemorate those who lost their lives in the Second World War.

The poignant memorials carry the names of more than 36,000 men and women who died at sea and have no known grave elsewhere.

Address: Trinity Square Gardens, Tower Hill, EC3N 4AA
Nearest tube: Tower Hill

● ●

9 April

VISIT JOHN WESLEY'S CHAPEL

The Father of Methodism, John Wesley, oversaw the building of a chapel on City Road in East London in 1778, as a replacement for the nearby foundery where he had previously been based.

Since then, the church has been a centre for the Methodist Church, and is also celebrated for its fine Georgian architecture. In 1984, a small museum was opened in the crypt, charting the history of Methodism from the 18th century to the present day.

www.wesleyschapel.org.uk
Address: 49 City Road, EC1Y 1AU
Nearest tubes: Old Street, Moorgate

GO GLIDING AT KENLEY AERODROME

A former **RAF** base which was one of three main stations responsible for the defence of London during the Second World War, Kenley Aerodrome is now home to the Surrey Hills Gliding Club, which offers trial sessions for budding glider pilots.

Flights can last anything from five to forty minutes, depending on the weather, and offer views across the green Surrey Hills, and the sprawl of South London to the North.

www.southlondongliding.co.uk

• •

11 April

Take a trip to Cambridgeshire

ON THE FEAST DAY OF ST GUTHLAC,
PATRON SAINT OF THE FENS

Marked only by a crooked lamppost on Hatton Garden, the Mitre is a small pub on tiny Ely Court in the City of London. On land which once fell within the grounds of the Palace of the Bishops of Ely, the current pub dates from around 1772, and is technically in Cambridgeshire.

Legend has it that the hidden alleyways in which the Mitre is situated have often been used by escaping criminals, as the City of London Police Force has no jurisdiction there.

Address: Ely Court, Hatton Garden, Holborn, EC1N 6SJ
Nearest tube: Chancery Lane, Farringdon

• •

12 April

Stock up on nautical supplies at Arthur Beale Ltd

Serving nautical visitors to the shop at 194 Shaftesbury Avenue for around 120 years, Arthur Beale is a traditional chandlers, selling rope, fittings, flags and other bits and bobs for boats.

It might seem an odd find in this area, where you wouldn't really expect to see such things, but this road is a hotbed for independent businesses, with both James Smith Umbrellas and the historic The Punjab restaurant nearby.

Address: 194 Shaftesbury Avenue, Covent Garden, WC2H 8JP
Nearest tubes: Covent Garden, Tottenham Court Road, Leicester Square

• •

13 April

EAT AT LONDON'S OLDEST INDIAN RESTAURANT

Veeraswamy is the UK's oldest surviving Indian restaurant, established at its present location in Regents Street in 1926 by the great-grandson of an English general and an Indian princess.

It has served countless customers over the years, including Charlie Chaplin, King Hussein of Jordan, Marlon Brando and former Indian premier Indira Gandhi.

www.veeraswamy.com
Address: 99 Regent Street, W1B 4RS
Nearest tubes: Piccadilly Circus, Oxford Circus

14 April

Explore a Tudor battlefield

Early in the morning on 14 April 1471, under cover of heavy mist, the Yorkist army of King Edward IV mounted a surprise attack on the Lancastrians to begin the Battle of Barnet, one of the decisive conflicts of the Wars of the Roses.

An obelisk on Hadley Green, in the North London village of Monken Hadley, was built in the 18th century to mark the location of the battle, and today the field is the only one in London to be protected by English Heritage's Register of Historic Battlefields.

Nearest tubes: High Barnet

15 April

Meet the Crystal Palace Sphinxes

When London hosted the Great Exhibition in 1851, it was a chance for London to show the world the power and greatness of Britain in the Victorian age. A vast Crystal Palace was built in Hyde Park as a place for more than 14,000 exhibitors, and no expense was spared on the architectural and design flourishes which were added.

When the Exhibition finished, the palace was relocated to Sydenham, and many of the sculptures and flourishes moved with it. The palace itself burned down in 1936, but some elements remain, including two sphinxes that keep watch over the empty terraces where once the palace stood.

Nearest rail: Crystal Palace

16 April

Eat fish and chips at Fish House

Often lauded as having amongst the best chips in London, Fish House, on Lauriston Road in Hackney, is an independent chippy opened by Gabriel Early and Johanna Nylander in June 2007, focusing on being a family-friendly local eatery.

Early and Nylander have been working together running various businesses in and around Victoria Park for ten years, and in 2006 they appeared in the Egon Ronay guide for their work at The Approach Tavern, in Bethnal Green.

www.fishouse.co.uk
Address: 126–128 Lauriston Road, E9 7LH
Nearest tube: Bethnal Green

17 April

Visit the Museum of Brands, Packaging and Advertising

Home to 12,000 items from some of the UK's most iconic brands, the Museum of Brands, Packaging and Advertising opened in Notting Hill in November 2005.

The Museum grew out of the collection of consumer historian Robert Opie, who began by saving a packet of Munchies chocolates at the age of 16, and has since collected around 300,000 items.

www.museumofbrands.com
Address: 2 Colville Mews, Lonsdale Road, Notting Hill, W11 2AR
Nearest tubes: Notting Hill Gate, Westbourne Park, Ladbroke Grove

18 April

Spend an evening at the Bookshop Theatre

The Calder Bookshop, otherwise known as the Bookshop Theatre, was established in 2000 by John Calder on The Cut in Waterloo.

The shop specialises in literary fiction, poetry and drama, but it also hosts discussions, literary readings, music events and theatre performances.

www.oneworldclassics.com/page.html?id=11
Address: 51 The Cut, SE1 8LF
Nearest tubes: Waterloo, Southwark

19 April

Examine the specimens at the Hunterian Museum

In 1799, the Government acquired the collection of surgeon John Hunter and gave it to the Royal College of Surgeons for the creation of a medical museum at their premises in Lincoln's Inn Fields.

The Museum hosts an amazing array of medical and zoological specimens, including the skeleton of a giant, various diseased bones and body parts, pickled frogs, deformed piglets and foetal skeletons. It is a fascinating, if somewhat grotesque, insight into the way our bodies work.

Address: The Royal College of Surgeons of England, 35–43 Lincoln's Inn Fields, WC2A 3PE
Nearest tubes: Holborn, Temple

20 April

Shop in the markets of Rye Lane

Home to various shops and stalls showcasing African meat, vegetables, clothes, textiles and spices, the shops along Rye Lane and the Rye Lane Indoor Market make the area one of London's most interesting shopping experiences.

Situated at the centre of one of London's most diverse areas, where nearly a third of people have African heritage, it's a fascinating place, and is another example of the rich variety of produce available in London.

Nearest rail: Peckham Rye

21 April

See the Crown Jewels

ON QUEEN ELIZABETH II'S BIRTHDAY

The Crown Jewels first came to call the Tower of London their home in 1303, when a theft led them to be moved from Westminster Abbey. Though there was a brief intermission when they were melted down upon the execution of Charles I, they were restored in 1660 and have been there ever since.

While some find the 23,578 gems that make up the Crown Jewels, and the diamond-encrusted Imperial State Crown, a little gaudy, seeing them is certainly an unforgettable experience.

www.hrp.org.uk/toweroflondon/stories/crownjewels.aspx
Address: The Tower of London, EC3N 4AB
Nearest tube: Tower Hill

22 April

Explore space at the Greenwich Planetarium

The Peter Harrison Planetarium, beside the Royal Observatory in Greenwich Park, is a 120-seater 'digital laser planetarium' which opened in 2007.

The Planetarium takes visitors on an audio-visual trip through time and space inside a £17.7 million 45-tonne bronze-clad cone, tilted at 51.5° to the horizontal (the latitude of Greenwich), and situated aptly on the prime meridian itself.

www.nmm.ac.uk/visit/planetarium-shows
Address: Royal Observatory, Blackheath Ave, SE10 8XJ
Nearest rail: Blackheath, Greenwich

23 April

Visit the church of St George in the East

ON ST GEORGE'S DAY

One of six 18th-century churches by Hawksmoor created under the New Churches in London & Westminster Act, St George in the East opened in 1729 when parts of the surrounding area were still semi-rural.

With the rise of Docklands, the green fields were soon swallowed up by the metropolis, and populations increased from around 300 houses in 1780 to nearly 49,000 at the time of the 1861 census. Today, the church serves a very diverse parish, made up of immigrant communities, lifelong East Enders and City professionals.

Address: Cannon Street Road, E1 0BH
Nearest tube: Shadwell

Notes

24 April

Buy Swedish at Totally Swedish

The Totally Swedish shop, on Crawford Street, combines a mission to offer a flavour of the motherland to the many Swedes who now call London home with spreading the word about Swedish food, children's products and handicrafts.

Founded in 2005 by Annethe Nathan and Teresia Bergsand, the shop opens up a world of Swedish cultural and culinary heritage to Londoners and expatriate Swedes.

www.totallyswedish.com
Address: 32 Crawford Street, W1H 1LS
Nearest tube: Baker Street

REMEMBER THE FALLEN AT THE NEW ZEALAND WAR MEMORIAL

ON ANZAC DAY

The New Zealand War Memorial, at Hyde Park Corner, remembers those from New Zealand who gave their lives in the First and Second World Wars. Mirroring its Australian cousin on the opposite side of the Wellington Arch, the Memorial, which was designed by architect John Hardwick-Smith and sculptor Paul Dibble, was completed in November 2006.

The Memorial is known as The Southern Stand and consists of sixteen large bronze cross-shaped 'standards', all set in the ground at an angle and facing south towards the Southern Hemisphere. Six of the standards are arranged in the shape of the Southern Cross.

Nearest tube: Hyde Park Corner

• •

26 April

CLIMB HORSENDEN HILL

Once home to an Iron Age settlement, Horsenden Hill rises to a modest height of 279 feet, and on a clear day there are views over six counties and ten London Boroughs from its summit.

Due to its strategic position, it played host to gun emplacements and a searchlight station during the major conflicts of the 20th century, but now is an altogether more sedate affair, popular with kite flyers and grazing Highlander cows.

Nearest rail: Sudbury & Harrow Road

27 April

Hire a deck chair

Deck chair season in the Royal Parks lasts from April until the end of September, offering comfortable chairs for a couple of pounds, and a chance to sit and watch the world go by.

Deck chairs are available in St James's Park, Regent's Park, Green Park and Hyde Park and in some places further afield.

www.royalparks.gov.uk

28 April

See the Berlin Wall

In the park just outside the Imperial War Museum is a genuine section of the Berlin Wall. Painted with the words 'Change Your Life', which are attributed to the graffiti artist Indiano, it originally stood near the Brandenburg Gate, one of eight Berlin Wall crossing points.

Following the Revolutions of 1989, and the fall of the Wall, it was at the Brandenburg Gate on 22 December 1989 that the crossing was officially reopened. The Museum acquired the section in 1991, two years after it fell.

www.iwm.org.uk
Address: Lambeth Road, SE1 6HZ
Nearest tubes: Lambeth North, Waterloo, Southwark

29 April

Walk in Sydenham Hill Wood

Sydenham Hill Wood is a nine-hectare area of ancient woodland in South London, and is the largest remaining tract of the old Great North Wood, which once stretched from Deptford to Selhurst.

The London Wildlife Trust have managed the site since 1982. As readers might imagine, wildlife abounds, but it is also interesting for the disused railway bed and tunnel which run through it, and a ruined folly which can be found among the trees.

www.southwark.gov.uk/info/461/a_to_z_of_parks/670/sydenham_
hill_wood/1
Address: Entrances at Sydenham Hill and Crescent Wood Road, SE26
Nearest rail: Forest Hill and Sydenham Hill

30 April

Visit Cecil Sharp House

Cecil Sharp House, just north of Regent's Park, is the home of the English Folk Dance and Song Society. The Society formed in 1932 when the Folk-Song Society and the English Folk Dance Society merged.

Today, the society holds regular dances, concerts and other events at the House, and there are also regular music, song and dancing classes. The Society hosts include Ceilidhs, barn dances and folk clubs, many suitable for all abilities from absolute beginners to the advanced, and all for a reasonable fee.

www.efdss.org

May

See the Deptford Jack

May Day has been marked by Jack in the Green ceremonies for generations, with large garlanded figures carried through the streets. London has had various Jacks over the years, and in Deptford the local Morris dancers resumed parading a Jack in the early 1980s, in the revival of a local tradition which dates from at least 1906.

The Jack is carried around Deptford, Greenwich and much of South-East London on May Day, and the Morris dancers dance to celebrate the coming summer.

www.deptford-jack.org.uk

WANDER WALTHAMSTOW MARSHES

Walthamstow Marshes is home to a wide array of wildlife, and is a Site of Special Scientific Interest. The area is home to species such as the internationally rare plant creeping marshwort and birds such as the reed bunting, sedge warbler and willow warblers.

In 1909, Alliott Verdon Roe completed the first all-British powered flight over the Marshes in a Roe I Triplane, which he built nearby, and today they are part of the Lee Valley Park, linking Hackney Marshes with the Walthamstow Reservoirs to the north.

www.leevalleypark.org.uk/en/content/cms/leisure/nature_reserves/walthamstow_marsh/
walthamstow_marsh.aspx
Address: Walthamstow Marshes, Lea Bridge Road, Leyton, London E10 7QL
Nearest tube: Leyton

....

....

....

....

....

....

3 May

Visit the Sikorski Museum

ON POLISH CONSTITUTION DAY

The Sikorski Museum was established in 1945 in memory of Polish General Sikorski to house his papers, and to commemorate the contribution of Polish forces during the Second World War. The annexation of Poland by the USSR had made it difficult for many Poles to return home and they wanted to ensure they had a museum in exile.

In 1946, the Museum's home in Kensington was purchased, and today the Polish Institute and Sikorski Museum operate from the site, housing the Museum's collections and archives, and a reference library for those studying Polish history.

www.pism.co.uk
Address: 20 Prince's Gate, SW7 1PT
Nearest tube: South Kensington

4 May

Get a snack at the Blackheath Tea Hut

Situated in the middle of Blackheath, on the side of the A2, the Blackheath Tea Hut may be small, but it serves scores of customers with tea and fresh snacks, cooked to order, 24 hours a day.

A simple menu of sandwiches, burgers and cakes is lapped up by all comers, and the Hut is a real institution in South-East London.

www.blackheath-tea-hut.co.uk
Address: Goffers Road, SE3 0UA
Nearest rail: Blackheath

5 May

Take the Marx and Engels pub crawl

ON KARL MARX'S BIRTHDAY

Given that Marxism had such an impact on global politics, it is easy to forget that the men behind the theory were fairly ordinary and at the end of a long day studying in the Reading Room of the British Museum, they liked a drink.

The pub crawls of Karl Marx and Friedrich Engels were legendary, as they rolled out of the British Museum to the Museum Tavern, then drank their way through the 18 pubs along Tottenham Court Road. Today, there are rather fewer, but the route is still a favourite pilgrimage for many, and the Museum Tavern is a great place to start.

6 May

Learn the history of Parliament at the Jewel Tower

The Jewel Tower, in Westminster, was built around 1365 and is one of only a handful of parts of the original medieval Royal Palace of Westminster.

Today, it is opened to the public by English Heritage and hosts a permanent exhibition charting the history of the Houses of Parliament from medieval times to the present day.

www.english-heritage.org.uk/daysout/properties/jewel-tower
Address: Abingdon Street, Westminster, SW1P 3JX
Nearest tube: Westminster

Take a tour by black cab

London has more than 20,000 licensed black cabbies, who have all had to demonstrate that they have 'The Knowledge' before they get their licence. As such, cabbies are often the best guides to London, and know many little nooks and crannies which most Londoners have never seen.

While there are a number of companies offering formal black cab tours, the best ones are to be had by befriending an ordinary cabbie, and asking if he might be available to show you round.

8 May

Play golf at Beckenham Place Park

Unlike the stuffy members-only golf clubs out in the wilds of Essex and Surrey, the Beckenham Place Park golf course, in South London, welcomes everyone to come and hit some balls under their 'pay and play' system.

With no membership – or expensive golf kit – required, players can turn up, hire clubs and shoes, pay and play. And if you're after some of that authentic '19th hole' atmosphere, the course has its own clubhouse, with bar and restaurant facilities.

www.glendale-golf.com/course-7-beckenham-place.aspx
Address: Beckenham Hill Road, Lewisham, BR3 5BP
Nearest rail: Beckenham Junction

9 May

Become a poet at Keats House

Keats House, in Hampstead, was home to the poet John Keats from 1818 to 1820, and is now maintained as a museum of his life and work.

The years he spent at the house were among the most productive of his life, and it was here that he fell in love with Fanny Brawne, the daughter of a neighbour, and wrote 'Ode to a Nightingale' under a plum tree in the garden.

www.keatshouse.cityoflondon.gov.uk
Address: Keats Grove, Hampstead, NW3 2RR
Nearest tube: Hampstead, Belsize Park

10 May

Visit the Design Museum

Founded in 1989 and in an old banana warehouse beside the Thames, the Design Museum claims to be the first museum of modern design.

With around 200,000 visitors a year, it isn't one of London's premier-league museums, but as an internationally recognised centre, it offers a brilliant insight into what is happening at the cutting edge of world design.

www.designmuseum.org
Address: Shad Thames, SE1 2YD
Nearest tubes: Tower Hill, Monument

11 May

Buy spices at the Spice Shop

Birgit Erath's Notting Hill Spice Shop grew from a tiny weekend stall on Portobello Market to a fully blown spice shop shop, opened in 1995.

Today it offers thousands of products, and is a popular spot for chefs from around London who come to buy her wares.

www.thespiceshop.co.uk
Address: 1 Blenheim Crescent, W11 2EE
Nearest tubes: Ladbroke Grove, Westbourne Park

12 May

Sit on the bench that ended slavery

A stone bench in the South London village of Keston marks the spot where William Wilberforce and Pitt the Younger came on 12 May 1787 to sit beneath an oak tree and debate the slave trade.

It was during that conversation that Pitt pressed Wilberforce to bring forth the bill that led to abolition, and though the oak has long since died, the bench was installed in 1862 by Earl Stanhope to honour the role of this spot, and the two men, in making the world a better place.

Nearest rail: Hayes rail station

13 May

Seek sustenance at the Pavilion Café, Dulwich Park

The Pavilion Café operates from a 115-year-old former cricket pavilion in Dulwich Park, offering a menu of fresh, often organic, dishes, and plenty of space to sit outside on a fresh May morning.

The café has been run by Tarka and Domani Cowlam since November 2002, and is open every day, with wireless internet, home-baked cakes, sandwiches and fresh food cooked on the premises.

Address: Dulwich Park, SE21 7BQ
Nearest rail: West Dulwich, North Dulwich

14 May

Explore the Camley Street Natural Park

Developed on the site of a coal yard which once held fuel for steam engines serving Kings Cross and St Pancras, the Camley Street Natural Park is a haven for wildlife alongside the Regents Canal.

The park covers two acres, and is managed by the London Wildlife Trust, with the help of staff and volunteers. It is used as an educational resource for schoolchildren, but is open to all.

www.wildlondon.org.uk/naturereserves/camleystreetnaturalpark
Address: 12 Camley Street, NW1 0PW
Nearest tubes: King's Cross, St Pancras

VISIT THE CLAREMONT LANDSCAPE GARDEN

Formerly part of the Claremont Estate, built by the architect Sir John Vanbrugh, the National Trust acquired the Claremont Landscape Garden, just outside Esher, in 1949. The garden shows examples of the work of great landscape gardeners such as Charles Bridgeman, William Kent and Lancelot 'Capability' Brown.

It is an estate of national importance, celebrated as an example of the English landscape style, and noted for its grass amphitheatre and cedar trees. At this time of year, the gardens are in full bloom, with rhododendrons and azaleas flowering and 50 acres of lakes, grottoes and vistas to explore.

www.nationaltrust.org.uk/main/w-claremontlandscapegarden
Address: Portsmouth Road, Esher, Surrey KT10 9JG
Nearest rail: Esher

16 May

BECOME A PHILOSOPHER AT THE SCHOOL OF LIFE

The School of Life, on Marchmont Street in Bloomsbury, is a social enterprise with a mission to get people to think more about how they live their lives.

Alongside a fascinating philosophical bookshop, the School also offers regular classes and workshops on everything from making the most of your spare time to getting your ideal job, peppered with philosophical insights from a diverse faculty.

www.theschooloflife.com
Address: 70 Marchmont Street, WC1N 1AB
Nearest tube: Russell Square

17 May

Attend a sale at Sotheby's

Famous for being the auction house of London's most wealthy, and rumoured to frequently dispose discreetly of wares owned by high-ranking Royals, Sotheby's dates from 1744, when London bookseller Samuel Baker held his first auction to dispose of the books of Sir John Stanley.

Today, it is a multi-million pound venture, but all of Sotheby's auctions are free and open to the public. It can be a great chance to get a sense of what the rich are buying, without any obligation to place a bid or part with any cash.

www.sothebys.com
Address: 34–35 New Bond Street, W1A 2AA
Nearest tubes: Bond Street, Oxford Circus

••••••••••••••••••••••••••••••••••••••

18 May

Walk in the Hermitage Riverside Memorial Garden

Created in memory of East End residents killed in the Second World War, the Hermitage Riverside Memorial Garden sits on the former site of Hermitage Wharf, which was destroyed in a firebomb raid in December 1940.

When the area came to be redeveloped in the late 1990s, the builders of a new block of flats nearby were made to create a memorial park as part of the planning agreement, and a memorial and riverside walkway were included to remember the civilians killed.

Nearest tube: Tower Hill

• •

19 May

Visit the Pumphouse Gallery

A Grade II-listed building in the heart of Battersea Park, the Pumphouse was built in 1861 to supply water to the lakes of Battersea Park. It fell derelict, but in 1986 restoration was begun by Wandsworth Council and English Heritage.

In 1992, it reopened as a shop, information centre and art gallery, before becoming a full-time gallery space in 1999. Today, it exhibits a range of works of arts and also acts as a venue for events, workshops, talks and film screenings.

www.pumphousegallery.org.uk
Address: Battersea Park, SW11 4NJ
Nearest rail: Battersea Park

• •

20 May

See the flowers of the English Garden

The English Garden, in Kennington Park, which was inspired by the designs of Britain's great garden designers such as Gertrude Jekyll and Inigo Triggs, opened in 1931.

The small garden is a restful place, full of suntraps; in late May, the lavender is just starting to come into flower, and the rose beds are rich in early colour. Some of London's ring-necked parakeets are occasional visitors, adding an exotic flair to the otherwise peaceful scene.

Address: Kennington Park Road, SE11 4BE
Nearest tube: Oval

21 May

Watch the birds on Crayford Marshes

The Thames path runs alongside Dartford Creek at Crayford Marshes, offering stunning views out towards the Queen Elizabeth Bridge. The area is a rare example of a grazing marsh in London; in May ponies roam, marsh warblers lurk in in the reedbeds, and cow parsley begins to bloom.

At low tide, wading birds feed in the rich mud along Dartford Creek, and around the Darent Flood Barrier, the raised path offers views along the Thames and back towards industrial Crayford, as well as to the green marshes of Rainham, across the Thames.

www.bexleyrspb.org.uk/reserves/crayford-marshes.php
Address: Best accessed from Forest Road, Slade Green
Nearest rail: Slade Green

22 May

Climb the Mabley Green Boulder

A huge piece of Cornish granite sits at the centre of Mabley Green in Hackney Wick and is sometimes used by practising climbers, and it has even hosted professional climbing classes in the past.

The boulder was placed here in 2008 as part of the Hackney Wick Festival as one half of an artwork called 'Boulder', by John Frankland, with the other half situated in Shoreditch.

www.hackney.gov.uk/reap-green-hackney-photo-gallery-22.htm

23 May

Pop by Boswell's Cafe

Boswell's Café, in Covent Garden, was opened as a tea house in 1725 and was popular with London's literati at the time. It takes its name from writer James Boswell who, at 7 pm on 16 May 1763, was sitting with owner Thomas Davies when Dr Samuel Johnson entered.

As a Scot, Boswell worried about meeting Johnson as he was famously said to have a dislike of the Scottish, but they became good friends and Boswell went on to write his famous biography, *The Life of Johnson*, and spent many years debating with him

www.boswells-coventgarden.co.uk
Address: 8 Russell Street, WC2B 5HZ

24 May

Admire the Victoria Memorial

ON EMPIRE DAY

Built of more than two thousand tons of white marble, the Victoria Memorial sits in front of Buckingham Palace as a testament to one of the most influential monarchs in British history.

Completed in 1911, designed by architect Sir Aston Webb, with the help of sculptor Sir Thomas Brock, the Memorial is so huge it is designated a Grade I-listed building, and plays a starring role in any state occasion.

Nearest tubes: Green Park, Victoria, St James Park

25 May

CYCLE THE GREENWAY

Stretching eastwards from Stratford and the Olympic Site to Beckton, the Greenway is an elevated cycle route which runs along the top of Joseph Bazalgette's Northern Outfall Sewer.

The traffic-free route offers views across industrial East London, passing lesser-visited areas such as Plaistow and Newham.

www.tfl.gov.uk/tfl/gettingaround/walkfinder

26 May

Take a trip on the Thames Clippers

Named after the fast sailing ships which transported tea around the world during the 19th century, the Thames Clippers are London's commuter boats, plying their trade on the Thames since the company was founded in 1999 by partners Sean Collins and Alan Woods.

Today, their high-speed catamarans carry 7,000 passengers a day, serving routes between Woolwich and Central London, including a dedicated service between the Tate Modern and the Tate Britain.

www.thamesclippers.com

27 May

Relax in the sun in the Glade

The Glade is a peaceful patch of grass at the Western end of Victoria Park, almost completely surrounded by trees and bushes.

It is home to various types of wildlife, including squirrels, woodpeckers and jays, and is a lovely place to enjoy a sunny day.

Nearest tube: Mile End

Notes

....

....

....

....

....

....

....

....

28 May

Climb Barn Hill

In the heart of the Brent suburbs is the Fryent Country Park, a 250-acre haven of rolling countryside which resisted the waves of Victorian industrialisation that consumed the areas around it.

At the southern end of the Park, Barn Hill rises to 86 metres above sea level, giving those at its summit a great vantage view of the 134-metre Wembley Arch just beyond. At this time of year the park is ablaze with yellow buttercups, making it particularly inviting.

www.bhcg.btck.co.uk

Sit beneath the Oak of Honor

ON ROYAL OAK DAY

Elizabeth I once picnicked beneath the Oak of Honor, the tree which stands on the summit of One Tree Hill, in South London. The tree was then part of the famous Great North Wood, which stretched from here along the ridge of the hill southwards towards Croydon.

While the original Oak has been lost, a newer version was planted in 1905, when the park was first opened to the public, and the importance of the tree is commemorated in both the name of the hill and the local area.

The hill offers beautiful views towards Central London and has attracted many artists to paint its scenes, but its strategic position also drew the Honourable East India Company, which used it as a signalling station during the Napoleonic Wars to get messages to the English Channel.

Nearest rail: Honor Oak Park

Explore Darwin's Down House

It was at Down House, near Orpington, that Charles Darwin spent most of his family life, from 1842 until his death in 1882. It was here that he wrote *The Origin of Species*, and conducted some of his most important work, both in his study and in his greenhouse and garden, where he kept his collection of Venus Flytraps.

Now maintained by English Heritage, Down House is a fascinating place to visit, giving insights into the life, work and intelligence of a man who helped us to understand who we are.

www.english-heritage.org.uk/daysout/properties/home-of-charles-darwin-down-house/
Address: Luxted Road, Downe, Kent BR6 7JT
Nearest rail: Bromley South

Visit St Lawrence Jewry

A pretty little church, right outside the Guildhall, St Lawrence Jewry was rebuilt after the Great Fire of London according to designs by Sir Christopher Wren. The church had been originally built in the 12th century, taking its name from the medieval Jewish ghetto which was once nearby.

Like a lot of City churches, not only was it destroyed in the Great Fire of London, but its rebuilt structure also suffered damage during the Second World War. It wasn't until 1957 that it was fully restored, in a way sympathetic to Wren's original design, probably because it had been designated a Grade I-listed structure in 1950.

www.stlawrencejewry.org.uk
Address: Guildhall Yard, EC2V 5AA
Nearest tube: St. Paul's, Mansion House

June

VISIT LEIGHTON HOUSE

On the edge of Holland Park in West London, Leighton House is a remarkable 19th-century building which was once home to the Victorian artist Lord Frederic Leighton.

Notable for its stunning pillared Arab Hall, which displays Leighton's priceless collection of Islamic tiles, it is now a museum of the Royal Borough of Kensington and Chelsea. The house hosts various exhibitions, and invites visitors to tour Leighton's studio.

www.rbkc.gov.uk/subsites/museums/leightonhousemuseum.aspx
Address: 12 Holland Park Road, W14 8LZ
Nearest tubes: High Street Kensington, Olympia, Holland Park

Relax in the shade of a London plane tree

Along the kerbsides of Central London, the London plane tree is ubiquitous, known for its tolerance of vehicle pollution, and its bright-green leaves which add colour to London scenes in summer.

The London plane is a hybrid of an Oriental plane and American plane, and grows up to 35 metres tall, with trunks of up to three metres in circumference.

Eat at Fatboy's Diner

Fatboy's Diner is an authentic American diner, built in 1941 in New Jersey, USA. It is now found at Trinity Buoy Wharf, in Docklands, just across the river from the O2.

The Diner specialises in burgers, breakfasts and milkshakes, and serves the surrounding businesses of Trinity Buoy Wharf, as well as hungry tourists.

www.fatboysdinerlondon.com
Address: Trinity Buoy Wharf, 64 Orchard Place, E14 0JW
Nearest DLR: East India

Learn to knit at I Knit

Founded as a friends knitting circle in 2005, I Knit opened on Lower Marsh, beside Waterloo Station, in 2008. The shop is a haven for knitters, stocking yarns, needles, crochet hooks and knitting books.

As well as offering a space to knit and chat instore, the shop takes knitting to new places, hosting the Knitting in Film and Television Awards, travelling to festivals and even developing Graffiti Knitting in the nearby Leake Street Tunnel.

www.iknit.org.uk
Address: 106 Lower Marsh, Waterloo, SE1 7AB
Nearest tubes: Waterloo, Lambeth North

Visit St Katharine's, the Danish Church

ON DANISH CONSTITUTION DAY

Since 1952, St Katharine's Church, near Regent's Park, has been a Danish church and cultural centre, offering a haven for Danes in London and an insight into the life and culture of Denmark.

The church holds regular services, film nights and Danish-language classes, as well as running a shop selling Danish food and drink. It also hosts a Danish book club, a mother and toddlers' group and Danish concerts.

www.danskekirke.org
Address: 4 St Katharine's Precinct, NW1 4HH
Nearest tubes: Camden Town

6 June

Visit the Harcourt, London's Swedish pub

ON THE NATIONAL DAY OF SWEDEN

The Harcourt is a pub situated a short distance from the Swedish Embassy in the same road as a Swedish church. It was inevitable, really, that the Harcourt would become London's Swedish pub.

Many of the bar staff are Swedish, and the pub sells Swedish cider, shows Swedish sports, hosts Swedish events and serves Swedish food.

www.theharcourt.com
Address: 32 Harcourt Street, W1H 4HX
Nearest tube: Edgware Road

7 June

Swim in Brockwell Lido

First opened in 1937, Brockwell Lido, in South London, is a popular lido housed within an Art Deco Grade II-listed building.

The Lido is a popular spot for a summertime swim, and has recently undergone a £3 million refurbishment, to ensure it is maintained for future generations of al fresco swimmers.

www.fusion-lifestyle.com/centres/Brockwell_Lido

8 June

Go sailing at the Docklands Sailing and Watersports Centre

Opened in 1989, the Docklands Sailing and Watersports Centre aims to provide recreational water activities for all sections of the community.

Maintained by full-time staff and volunteers, the centre offers a range of adult and youth courses and open sessions, including Wednesday-night twilight sails, where sailing is mixed with long evenings and a barbecue.

www.dswc.org
Address: 235a Westferry Road, Isle of Dogs, E14 3QS
Nearest tube: Canary Wharf

9 June

Visit Charles Dickens' House

ON DICKENS DAY (DATE OF DICKENS' DEATH)

The Charles Dickens Museum, situated at 48 Doughty Street, was Charles Dickens's home from 1837 until 1839. It was here that the great man completed and published *The Pickwick Papers*, *Oliver Twist* and *Nicholas Nickleby*.

The building is Dickens's only surviving London home and was opened as a museum in 1925. It is now home to an important collection of rare editions, paintings, manuscripts, furniture and other Dickens-based items.

www.dickensmuseum.com
Address: 48 Doughty Street, WC1N 2LX
Nearest tubes: Russell Square, Chancery Lane, Holborn

10 June

PLAY PÉTANQUE AT HAY'S GALLERIA

The traditional French game of pétanque has struggled to make inroads in London, possibly due to the unpredictable climate. There are a few pitches, however, and one which does not suffer from meteorological problems is at Hay's Galleria, in Southwark.

Covered by the high roof of the arcade, it is owned by Balls Brothers, an upmarket wine-bar chain, and is free to hire.

http://venues.ballsbrothers.co.uk/petanque/index.htm
Address: Hay's Galleria, 55A Tooley Street, SE1 2QN
Nearest tube: London Bridge

11 June

Eat at the Passage Café

The Passage Café in Clerkenwell is a lovely little French bistro run by Katarina and Pascal Brunet. In summer, tables spill out of the tiny café on to the street outside, giving it a continental feel.

A single waitress makes everyone feel like they are very important, and rushes around, creating a lively French atmosphere, with the walls sporting a good mix of Toulouse Lautrec prints, vintage Ricard ads and impressionist artworks.

www.thepassagecafe.com
Address: 12 Jerusalem Passage, EC1V 4JP
Nearest tubes: Chancery Lane, Barbican

12 June

Explore the Royal Academy's Summer Exhibition

The Royal Academy's Summer Exhibition is held every year at the Academy's Burlington House, on Piccadilly. It is the largest open contemporary art exhibition in the world, offering an interesting insight into the modern art world.

The exhibition has been running since 1769, when it began in a warehouse on Pall Mall, and today it draws together a huge range of new works by various artists, curated by a rotating committee of Royal Academicians, with different people curating the rooms.

www.royalacademy.org.uk/
Address: Royal Academy of Arts, Burlington House, Piccadilly W1J 0BD
Nearest tubes: Piccadilly Circus, Green Park

13 June

Buy fish at Billingsgate Market

Billingsgate Market has been London's fish market since the sixteenth century, when the riverside market became established at Billingsgate Wharf. In the nineteenth century, the Market moved to Lower Thames Street, before relocating to Docklands in the 1980s.

Today, the country's largest inland fish market sells fish five days a week, opening at 5 am and trading until 8.30 am. Live crabs share stalls with huge tuna and conger eels, whilst the Asian and African specialists stock exotic fish from around the world.

www.billingsgate-market.org.uk
Address: Billingsgate Market, Trafalgar Way, E14 5ST
Nearest tube/DLR: Canary Wharf, Poplar, West India Quay

Sit in the St Dunstan church in the East Public Garden

St Dunstan-in-the-East was a rather unlucky church: severely damaged in the Great Fire of London, it had been rebuilt twice, once to plans by Sir Christopher Wren, and again in 1817 after falling into disrepair. When it was damaged again during the Second World War, it stood untouched until 1967, and the decision was taken not to rebuild it.

The church now lives on one of the most beautiful public gardens in the City of London, with greenery, climbers and creepers covering the ruins and occasional church services held in the open air.

www.ahbtt.org.uk/history/st-dunstan-in-the-east/
Address: St Dunstan's Hill, EC3
Nearest tube: Monument, Tower Hill

Enjoy a cuppa in Kennington Park café

Kennington Park's beautiful Victorian cafe is an Arts and Crafts 'refreshment house' which is still in use today. Its attractive setting at the heart of the park makes it a popular spot in summer. Originally designed by architects at London County Council and installed in 1897, it is now Grade II-listed by English Heritage and serves a great cup of tea.

www.kenningtonpark.org/cafe

Have a drink on the Wibbley Wobbley

The Wibbley Wobbley is a floating pub in Greenland Dock, South-East London, with an upstairs restaurant. Located in a converted barge, it is pleasant spot for a drink, with views out across the Dock.

It is a real community pub, with interesting local and nautical pub paraphernalia inside, a noticeboard filled with local information, and a friendly pub cat who is keen to meet new people.

Address: Greenland Dock, off Rope St, Surrey Quays, SE16 7SZ
Nearest tube: Surrey Quays

17 June
Visit Nunhead Cemetery

One of a ring of great Victorian cemeteries created around what was once the outskirts of London, Nunhead Cemetery was consecrated in 1840 and covers 52 acres of South London. Known for its meandering paths, its architectural details include an octagonal gothic chapel designed by Thomas Little.

Now maintained by the formidable Friends of Nunhead Cemetery, the grounds have been the subject of extensive restorations over the last 30 years to return them to a fitting tribute to those buried there, and a peaceful place for a walk on a summer's evening.

www.fonc.org.uk
Address: Linden Grove, London SE15 3LW
Nearest rail: Nunhead

THINGS TO DO TODAY:

18 June
Admire a Waterloo sunset

ON WATERLOO DAY

Named to commemorate the British victory in the Battle of Waterloo, the original Waterloo Bridge opened on 18 June 1817, and its name was adopted for the terminus of the London and South Western Railway when it was completed in 1848.

In the evenings, the station and bridge are always busy with commuters, and more than eighty million pass through each year. The bridge, which famously inspired lovers Terry and Julie in the Kinks' 1967 hit 'Waterloo Sunset', is a spectacular place to watch the sun set over the river.

Nearest tube: Waterloo

19 June
Visit Strawberry Hill

Adapted from a smaller property in the mid-18th century by Horace Walpole, Strawberry Hill in Twickenham was the world's first Gothic revival house.

Walpole originally bought Strawberry Hill as a small villa, and subsequently doubled its size, expanded the plot from 5 to 46 acres and added towers and battlements. The 'little gothic castle' had a significant impact on subsequent architecture, influencing Gothic revival buildings such as the Houses of Parliament, St Pancras Station and Tower Bridge.

www.strawberryhillhouse.org.uk
Address: Strawberry Hill, 268 Waldegrave Road, Twickenham TW1 4ST
Nearest rail: Strawberry Hill

....

....

....

....

....

....

....

....

....

....

20 June

Watch the sunrise on Primrose Hill

Primrose Hill rises 256 feet above sea level at the north end of Regent's Park, and for many years has been the unofficial centre of midsummer celebrations in London, as people gather in the early morning to mark the midpoint of the year.

The hill is formed of London clay, and was once part of Henry VIII's hunting ground. It was not officially designated as public space until 1842. Around the solstice, it often attracts Druids and casual sun-worshippers seeking midsummer sun.

Nearest tubes: Chalk Farm, Camden Town, St John's Wood

21 June

Listen to a concert in Embankment Gardens

In the summer months, Westminster City Council hosts an annual season of free concerts at its open air bandstand in Embankment Gardens, with music varying from jazz and brass bands to travelling choirs and school groups.

Attendance is free, and concerts take place at lunchtimes, attracting a mixed crowd of tourists, pensioners and accountants and civil servants from the surrounding offices.

www.westminster.gov.uk/services/environment/landandpremises/
parksandopenspaces/veg/
Nearest tubes: Embankment, Temple

22 June

Play Pitch and Putt on Palewell Common

The Pitch and Putt course at Palewell Common, East Sheen, offers a welcome opportunity for London's amateur golfers to test their strokes in open space.

While the course is limited to only nine short holes, its full-size greens offer welcome practice space for those looking to sharpen their putting skills.

www.pitchnputt.co.uk/course%20pages/course%20details%20
palewell.htm

• •

23 June

SPEND A NIGHT UNDER CANVAS AT LEE VALLEY CAMPSITE

The Lee Valley Campsite offers a rare opportunity to spend a night in a tent or caravan within the M25 for a reasonable fee.

From the campsite, it is possible to walk to Chingford Station, for trains to Central London, but also to the walking and picnicking spots of Epping Forest, and along the canal towpaths of the Lee Valley Park.

www.leevalleypark.org.uk/en/content/cms/where_to_stay/campsite_sewardstone/campsite_sewardstone.aspx
Address: Lee Valley Campsite, Sewardstone Road, Chingford, E4 7RA
Nearest tube: Walthamstow Central

24 June

Admire Queen Mary's Rose Garden

ON MIDSUMMER DAY

Home to 30,000 plants of 400 varieties, London's largest collection of roses is found in Queen Mary's Rose Garden, in Regent's Park.

Added in 1932, the Garden is situated on the Inner Circle, a location which was previously home to the Royal Botanic Society, and it was one of the last parts of the Park to be opened to the public.

www.royalparks.gov.uk/The-Regents-Park.aspx
Nearest tubes: Great Portland Street, Baker Street, St John's Wood

25 June

Explore George Orwell's Hampstead

ON HIS BIRTHDAY

Author George Orwell spent at least two years living in Hampstead, working part-time in a bookshop called Booklover's Corner, in South End Road, from 1934 to 1935, and sharing a flat at 50 Lawford Road from August 1935 until early 1936.

Some of his experiences there are recounted in his novel, *Keep the Aspidistra Flying*, first published in 1936, which charts his time in suburbia, struggling for money to live as a writer, and fighting a battle against the Money God, which becomes all-pervading. His presence is also marked by memorials at both the addresses, though the bookshop sadly no longer exists.

26 June

Go camping at Wimbledon

Every day during Wimbledon, a number of tickets are set aside for people willing to turn up on the day, and in order to get there early enough, many resort to camping overnight.

The queuing system for on-day tickets is designed to ensure fairness. Camping is positively encouraged, but, if you do choose to, you'll be woken around 6 am by stewards and asked to dismantle any camping equipment to create space for those joining the queue on the day.

www.wimbledon.com
Nearest tubes: Southfields, Wimbledon

27 June

Sit on Ian Dury's Bench

A wooden park bench dedicated to the singer Ian Dury can be found in Poet's Corner, in the Pembroke Lodge Gardens area of Richmond Park, inscribed with his 'Reasons to be Cheerful' lyric.

The seat was installed in 2002, and features a headphone socket where visitors can plug in and hear some of Dury's songs and an interview with him, though it has sometimes been the subject of vandalism.

Nearest tube: Richmond

28 June
Go for a paddle at the V&A

We all like a bit of culture, but in June we do occasionally want a break outside and, if facilities permit, have a bit of a paddle. At the V&A's John Madejski Garden, you can combine all three, but it's mostly about the paddling.

Opened in July 2005, the garden, designed by Kim Wilkie, is in the impressive surroundings of the V&A's Italianate central courtyard, and features at its centre a stone-paved oval, with surrounding steps and water jets, which is either filled with water as a paddling pool, or drained for displays.

Usually filled at the weekends, it is a beautiful, communal use of the £2 million given by Mr Madejski, specifically to create the new garden at the heart of the Museum.

www.vam.ac.uk/page/j/john-madejski-garden
Address: Cromwell Road, SW7 2RL
Nearest tube: South Kensington

29 June
Explore East London by canoe

Canoes are available to hire from Lee Valley Canoe Cycle in Tottenham by the day, hour or week. If you're in the mood for a full day, the centre is only around five miles from the Olympic site, and canoeists have been known to do the full round trip, carrying the canoes over the locks of the River Lee Navigation.

Despite expectations of Dickensian canals filled with all sorts of horrors, today's waterways are considerably cleaner – and you will probably only see a few rats, and end up with a wet leg or two. Canoeists should come equipped with strong arms if they are intending to carry the canoe over locks, as well as their best waving arms, as everyone seems a lot more friendly when you're travelling by canal.

www.lvcc.biz
Address: The Watersedge, Stonebridge Lock, Tottenham Marshes, London N17 0XD
Nearest rail: Tottenham Hale

30 June

See Dulwich Park
by pedal power

London Recumbents, in Dulwich Park, have been hiring some of South London's most interesting cycles to Londoners since 1993, and they have proven very popular with families and young people visiting the park.

The company has a variety of interesting pedal-powered contraptions, including recumbent tricycles, family tandems and some side-by-side tandem tricycles, hired out daily for use on the acres of flat space available in the park.

www.londonrecumbents.com
Address: Ranger's Yard, Dulwich Park, SE21 7BQ
Nearest rail: North Dulwich, West Dulwich

July

1 July

Walk over the Mile End Green Bridge

Traversing the A11 at a busy junction in East London, the Mile End Green Bridge was created by architect Piers Gough to ensure that both sides of the 90-acre Mile End Park were connected without a break. As well as the road, a line of shops operates from beneath the bridge.

The bridge was built following a £12.3 million grant from the Millennium Commission, and each day 75,000 cars pass beneath it, taking little notice of the grassy park above them.

Nearest tube: Mile End

2 July

Visit Mayfield Lavender Farm

Although lavender is a fickle flower, it usually gives a brilliant display of colour by early July, and Mayfield Lavender Farm, outside Banstead in South London, is the best place to witness it.

Though the area was once one of the country's most important for lavender farming, today Mayfield Farm is a relative rarity, and that is what makes it such a brilliant place to visit. The stark colours of the farm also make it a great place for photographers, and the owners run a yearly photography competition for visitors.

www.mayfieldlavender.com
Address: Croydon Lane, Banstead, Surrey SM7 3BE

3 July

Take a dip in the Berkeley's rooftop pool

At the top of one of London's most exclusive hotels, offering panoramic views over Mayfair and Hyde Park, the Berkeley Hotel's rooftop pool is a pretty special spot, and even on days where the sun is unreliable, the specially designed roof sliding roof will protect you from the elements.

Thankfully, you don't always have to be a guest to take advantage of the unique pool and on some days the hotel offers full- or half-day Berkeley Health Club and Spa membership, allowing access to non-residents.

www.the-berkeley.co.uk
Address: Wilton Place, Knightsbridge, SW1X 7RL
Nearest tubes: Knightsbridge, Hyde Park Corner

4 July

Drink on the spot where America began

ON AMERICAN INDEPENDENCE DAY

The Mayflower in Rotherhithe is a stone's throw from the quay where the *Mayflower* ship docked in London before its departure for the New World.

While the current pub is from a later date, there was almost certainly a pub on the site when the Pilgrim Fathers walked the quayside, though they may not have made use of it themselves.

Address: 117 Rotherhithe Street, Rotherhithe, SE16 4NF
Nearest tube: Rotherhithe

5 July

Swim outside in Hackney

In the heart of Hackney, the London Fields Lido is an excellent outdoor pool which was once threatened by bulldozers. It is very popular with all ages, owing to its heating, which regulates water temperatures around 25°C.

Originally built in 1932, it remained open, apart from the war years, until its closure in 1988. Then closed for 18 years, a local campaign secured its future, and it reopened in 2006. The pool is Olympic-sized, measuring 50 metres by 17 metres, and is open to the public every day.

www.hackney.gov.uk/c-londonfields-lido.htm
Address: London Fields Westside, E8 3EU
Nearest rail: London Fields

• •

6 July

Become a groundling at the Globe Theatre

When Sam Wanamaker's team finally realised its dream of recreating Shakespeare's Globe Theatre, on the South Bank, it was keen to ensure the experience was as faithful as possible to how people would have watched plays 400 years ago.

Every show offers a limited number of cheap tickets to 'groundlings' who stand in the yard. While often only those with the strongest legs can manage an entire show, it is a truly magical way to watch a play, beneath the open sky. Those who survive are always proud of their achievement.

www.shakespearesglobe.com
Address: 21 New Globe Walk, SE1 9DT
Nearest tubes: Mansion House, London Bridge

· ·

7 July

SEE THE DAGENHAM WIND TURBINES

Rising 85 metres above the Dagenham estate of the Ford Motor Company in East London are two huge wind turbines.

Completed in April 2004 by green energy company Ecotricity, they mark the first wind farm to be built in London, and at full capacity each turbine generates enough electricity to power 1,200 homes.

8 July
Picnic beside the Serpentine

Since Victorian times, Hyde Park has been one of London's most popular picnicking spots, and the area to the north of the Serpentine – where trees and green lawns roll down towards the lake – is one of the best spots to spend an afternoon.

With plenty of space, and legendary purveyors of Royal picnic baskets Fortnum & Mason only a short hop away, it is hard to imagine a better spot. The park keepers have even laid on rowing boats and toilets to provide for after-picnic needs.

www.royalparks.gov.uk/Hyde-Park.aspx

9 July
Wander in the Phoenix Garden

The Phoenix Garden is a community garden located just behind the Phoenix Theatre in Central London. Designed to give people working in the West End a green retreat, it offers a chance to see some nature, and is a great spot to retreat to when the summer heat starts to make life uncomfortable.

Started in 1984, the garden is still maintained by the same volunteer organisation that created it on the site of an old car park, which had previously been a Second World War bombsite.

www.phoenixgarden.org
Address: Entrance is on St Giles Passage
Nearest tubes: Tottenham Court Road, Leicester Square

10 July
Take a Fat Tire Bike Tour

Fat Tire Bike Tours depart daily from just outside Queensway Tube Station for a four-hour tour of Royal London, which takes in Buckingham Palace, Hyde Park, Kensington Gardens, the Houses of Parliament and Westminster Abbey.

This is possibly one of London's safest areas to cycle as you rarely have to leave the parks. Even so, the cost of the tour includes an optional helmet and reflective vest to maximise safety.

http://fattirebiketours.com/london
Nearest tube: Queensway

11 July
Visit William Morris's Red House

Owned by the National Trust, Red House, in Bexleyheath, was commissioned, built and lived in by designer, artist and writer William Morris. When Morris was forced to sell the house for financial reasons, it became a family home for nearly 140 years, then passed to the National Trust in 2002.

Though completed in 1860, its Arts and Crafts interior gives it a much earlier feel, as does its red brick-and-tile domestic vernacular style, which focuses on natural materials. The Grade I-listed building offers many gems of Arts and Crafts design, and is noted for its peaceful gardens and beautiful stairway.

www.nationaltrust.org.uk/main/w-redhouse
Address: Red House Lane, Bexleyheath, Kent DA6 8JF
Nearest rail: Bexleyheath

Take a dip in Hampstead Bathing Ponds

Though Hampstead Heath's three swimming ponds are notable for being the only life-guarded open-water swimming facilities in the UK which open to the public every day all year round, summer is definitely the best time for unaccustomed swimmers to take a dip.

The three ponds – the Mixed Pond, the Men's Pond and the Ladies' Pond – were originally dug and dammed in the 17th and 18th centuries as reservoirs and were only formalised as swimming ponds much later. Though water quality is monitored regularly to ensure quality, those who remain sceptical of pond swimming have a fine alternative in the form of the nearby Parliament Hill Lido.

Nearest tube: Hampstead

13 July

Enjoy a night at the opera in Holland Park

Opera first became a summertime staple in Holland Park in the late 1980s, and the popular season has been a West London hit ever since. With the help of resident orchestra, the City of London Sinfonia, the company puts on a number of productions each year.

Since 2007, the comfortable theatre has had a 1,600-square metre roof designed to protect the audience – if necessary – from the elements, while maintaining acoustics, and there are even pre-bookable picnics available on request.

www.rbkc.gov.uk/subsites/operahollandpark.aspx
Address: Entrance to the park is via Ilchester Place Gate, The Duchess of Bedford Gate or from Holland Walk and Holland Park Avenue
Nearest tubes: High Street Kensington, Holland Park

14 July

Drink at The French House

ON BASTILLE DAY

Originally called The York Minster, it wasn't until the Second World War that The French House took on its French style, attracting crowds of free French soldiers. It is even said that Charles De Gaulle wrote his famous speech, '*À tous les Français*' in the pub.

The French House subsequently became popular with local artists and writers, with patrons including Dylan Thomas and Francis Bacon. Still known for its gallic stubbornness, it refuses to serve beer in pint glasses.

www.frenchhousesoho.com
Address: 49 Dean Street, Soho, W1D 5BG
Nearest tube: Leicester Square, Piccadilly Circus, Covent Garden

WATCH A SHOW AT THE REGENT'S PARK OPEN AIR THEATRE

ON ST SWITHUN'S DAY

The 1,240-seat Open Air Theatre in Regent's Park has been putting on productions every summer since 1932, and underwent a £2 million rebuilding project in 1999, with designs by Haworth Tompkins Architects.

While the seats and stage are in the open air, the theatre makes a point of never cancelling a show before the start time due to poor weather, and completes 94 per cent of performances each year.

www.openairtheatre.org
Address: Entry is via the box office in Queen Mary's Garden within Regent's Park.
Nearest tube: Baker Street

16 July

WALK IN THE TREETOPS

The Rhizotron and Xstrata Treetop Walkway, at Kew Gardens, allows visitors to climb 59 feet up into the tree canopy and examine the foliage from an entirely new vantage point.

Opened to the public in 2008, the walkway was designed by the same architects who created the London Eye and is based on a Fibonacci numerical sequence, one of nature's common growth patterns.

www.kew.org
Address: Kew, Richmond, Surrey TW9 3AB
Nearest tube: Kew Gardens

17 July

Lie on the beach at Ruislip Lido

London's only public beach can be found at the heart of a national nature reserve beside Ruislip Lido lake, in Ruislip Woods, West London.

Dug in 1811 to feed water to the Grand Union Canal, it is now a popular spot for West Londoners going for picnics and walks and even has a narrow gauge railway taking visitors along the shore.

www.hillingdon.gov.uk/index.jsp?articleid=11103

18 July

Find Nelson Mandela in Parliament Square

ON HIS BIRTHDAY

In 2007, Nelson Mandela came to Parliament Square to witness the unveiling of a statue of his likeness, recalling how he and his friend Oliver Tambo had visited in the early 1960s and joked that one day a black person would join the statue of the former South African leader General Jan Smuts in the square.

The nine-foot figure is a realisation of that dream, with Mandela in a trademark flowery shirt, joining great figures like Abraham Lincoln and Winston Churchill at the heart of our democracy.

www.london.gov.uk/parliamentsquare/index.jsp
Nearest tubes: Westminster, St James's Park

19 July

Catch the Shepperton Ferry

The Shepperton Ferry has been helping people cross the Thames between Shepperton and Weybridge for around 500 years, and even famously featured in H. G. Wells' *War of the Worlds*.

Today, the ferry helps provide an important link on the Thames Path, allowing walkers and cyclists coming from London to continue their journey to Shepperton Lock and out towards the M25. The ferry runs every 15 minutes and a bell is provided to be rung on the quarter hour to alert the ferryman that you are waiting.

20 July

Visit Pitzhanger Manor

Pitzhanger Manor, in Ealing's Walpole Park, is a cultural venue, contemporary art space and historical house originally built in the 17th century, and partially rebuilt by owner and architect John Soane between 1800 and 1804.

By 1900, it had been acquired by Ealing Council and in 1987 it became the London Borough of Ealing's museum, known as the PM Gallery & House.

Address: PM Gallery & House, Walpole Park, Mattock Lane, W5 5EQ
Nearest tube: Ealing Broadway

21 July

EAT AT BABYLON

The Babylon Restaurant, on the 7th floor of 99 Kensington High Street, was opened in 2001 and has been a popular spot with West Londoners ever since, even winning the Visit London Best Restaurant Award in 2008.

The restaurant overlooks the Kensington Roof Gardens, laid out by landscape architect Ralph Hancock in the years before the Second World War. The gardens are an amazing sight, with hundreds of species of plant, and even a flamingo pond, visible from the restaurant's terrace.

www.roofgardens.virgin.com
Address: 99 Kensington High Street, W8 5SA
Nearest tube: High Street Kensington

22 July

Drink at the Duke of Kendal

A welcoming local pub, just a short distance from Marble Arch, the Duke of Kendal is just around the corner from Tony Blair's grand Georgian home, but is a welcoming spot with a loyal local clientele.

Known for its popular music nights, which culminate every week in a Sunday night singalong around the piano, the pub takes its name from Charles Stuart, son of James II, who tragically died before his first birthday.

http://dukeofkendal.tripod.com
Address: 38 Connaught Street, W2 2AF
Nearest tube: Marble Arch

● ●

23 July

Visit the MCC Cricket Museum

The MCC Cricket Museum at Lord's Cricket Ground is the world's oldest sporting museum and is the permanent home of the original Ashes urn.

The Museum tells the story of cricket from W. G. Grace to Alastair Cook through pictures, cartoons, bats and balls and other artefacts which the club has collected since 1864.

www.lords.org/history/mcc-museum
Address: St John's Wood, NW8 8QN

24 July

Discover the art of garden at Painshill Park

Created in the 18th century by Charles Hamilton, an aristocrtatic painter and designer, Painshill Park sits just inside the M25 at Cobham in Surrey.

The huge park is notable for its many follies, which include a Gothic temple and tower, a Turkish tent, a Chinese bridge and a crystal grotto.

www.painshill.co.uk
Address: Portsmouth Road, Cobham, Surrey KT11 1JE
Nearest tube: Cobham

25 July

See Queen Elizabeth's Hunting Lodge

Found on the edge of Epping Forest – once a Royal hunting ground – Queen Elizabeth's Hunting Lodge was actually built for Henry VIII in 1543.

The lodge offered a grandstand to enable guests to view the hunt from a high vantage point, and even participate with crossbows. Today, it is open to visitors, allowing them to get a flavour of what life was like in Tudor times.

Address: Queen Elizabeth's Hunting Lodge, Rangers Road,

Chingford E4 7QH
Nearest rail: Chingford

26 July

Relax at the London Peace Pagoda

The London Peace Pagoda, beside the Thames in Battersea Park, was built in 1985, after the monks and nuns of the Nipponzan Myohoji Buddhist Order came to London and lived within the park.

Wandsworth Council eventually offered them a storeroom, in the trees near the Old English Garden, on the understanding they carried out all renovations and the conversion into a temple, and the Pagoda was built nearby.

www.batterseapark.org/html/pagoda.html
Nearest rail: Battersea Park

27 July

Enjoy a cuppa beside Stoke Newington's West Reservoir

The café at the Stoke Newington West Reservoir Water Sports Centre is a lovely spot, affording visitors an opportunity to spend an hour sunning themselves on a deck beside the reservoir and watching the boats sailing by.

This is a picturesque corner of Stoke Newington, attracting only those in the know, and sailing schoolchildren eager to splash each other with reservoir water. For adults, however, it is a more sedate place to relax with a book and a cuppa.

www.gll.org/centre/stoke-newington-west-reservoir-centre.asp
Address: Green Lanes, Hackney, N4 2HA
Nearest tube: Manor House

EXPLORE THE WELL HALL PLEASAUNCE

Dating back to the 13th century, Eltham's Well Hall Pleasaunce is a formal garden containing flowers, ponds, woodland and a Tudor barn which is now a restaurant.

The gardens were once part of the estate of Well Hall House, home of *Railway Children* creator E. Nesbit, and still contain the house's kitchen garden, medieval bridge and formal Italian garden.

www.wellhall.org.uk
Address: Well Hall Road, SE9 6SZ
Nearest rail: Eltham

● ●

29 July

POP IN TO THE PALM TREE, MILE END

An atmospheric relic of the old East End, the Palm Tree pub sits alone in a park beside the Regents Canal in Mile End.

On summer evenings customers spread out on the grass beside the canal, but the pub is at its best when live bands strike up a tune at weekends, and well-dressed regulars mix with East London youngsters to soak up the lively atmosphere.

Address: 127 Grove Road, E3 5BH
Nearest tubes: Mile End, Stepney Green

30 July

See the houseboats of Taggs Island

Just up river from Hampton Court, Taggs Island has long been a haven for houseboaters, and this was expanded after the island's hotel was demolished in 1971, and a new lagoon was created at the island's centre.

Author J. M. Barrie and actor Charlie Chaplin are both thought to have spent time on the boats in the island's earlier days and more recently musician Dave Gilmour converted one into a studio to record the Pink Floyd albums *A Momentary Lapse of Reason* and *The Division Bell*.

31 July

Go for a walk around Alexandra Palace

Often overlooked by those unwilling to stray to North London, Alexandra Palace was built using materials from the Great Exhibition in Hyde Park and finished in 1873. Once home to the BBC, it was from here that the world's first TV broadcasts were made, and it also acted as a prisoner of war camp during the First World War.

Today, the 'People's Palace' plays host to various exhibitions and concerts, and the 196 acres of parkland which surround it include a pitch-and-putt golf course, a garden centre, a boating lake and a deer enclosure.

www.alexandrapalace.com
Address: Alexandra Palace Way, N22 7AY
Nearest tube: Wood Green

August

1 August

Wander Middlesex Filter Beds

Now a nature reserve, which is part of the Lee Valley Regional Park, the original six Middlesex Filter Beds were created in 1852 in order to purify water for the surrounding areas and prevent cholera, and operated until 1969.

In the 1980s, seven beds were leased to the Lee Valley Regional Park to form a nature reserve which is today home to over sixty different species of bird, including snipe, reed warblers and sparrowhawk, and also amphibians such as toads, frogs and newts.

www.leevalleypark.org.uk/EN/default.aspx?n1=3&n2=65&n3=67
Nearest rail: Clapton

Notes

....

....

....

....

....

....

....

2 August

Eat at Rules, London's oldest restaurant

Founded by Thomas Rule in 1798, Rules, on Maiden Lane in Covent Garden, is London's oldest restaurant. It was established when Mr Rule made a promise to his family that he would say goodbye to his wayward past and settle down, and opened it as an Oyster Bar, serving British cuisine.

During its history, Rules has entertained many famous names, including John Galsworthy, H.G. Wells, Henry Irving, Laurence Olivier and John Betjeman, who described the interior as 'unique and irreplaceable, and part of literary and theatrical London', and helped save it from demolition in the 1970s.

www.rules.co.uk
Address: 35 Maiden Lane, Covent Garden, WC2E 7LB
Nearest tubes: Charing Cross, Covent Garden, Leicester Square

Admire the view from Stave Hill

Stave Hill is an artificial mound created in the 1980s overlooking the Russia Dock Woodland in Rotherhithe. The hill is conical and rises 30 feet, with steps up one side leading to a viewing platform and a bronze relief map of the docks.

Nearby Russia Dock and Stave Dock, originally key parts of the Surrey Commercial Docks which were filled in the 1980s, were redeveloped by the London Docklands Development Corporation. Russia Dock became the site of a woodland and eco park.

Nearest tube: Rotherhithe

4 August

Visit the Serpentine Pavillion

Every year since 2000, the Serpentine Gallery has built a temporary pavillion in Hyde Park between July and October as a showcase for modern architecture and design.

Previous designers have included Iraqi-British architect Zaha Hadid, Norwegian architect Kjetil Thorsen, Swiss architect Peter Zumthor and Brazilian Oscar Niemeyer.

www.serpentinegallery.org
Address: Serpentine Gallery, Kensington Gardens, W2 3XA
Nearest tubes: Lancaster Gate, Knightsbridge, South Kensington

5 August

Explore the Sexby Garden

At the centre of Peckham Rye Park, the Sexby Garden is a formal garden named after horticulturist Lt-Colonel J.J. Sexby, who designed the park's original English Flower Garden. It was later renamed the Sexby Garden in his honour.

The Garden is set out in a formal style, with a range of plants and shrubs, as well as fountains, paving and pergola structures, and benches around its edge.

Nearest rail: East Dulwich, Nunhead, Peckham Rye

6 August

Swim on a rooftop at Oasis

One of the most central public leisure centres, the Oasis — previously known as Endell Baths — is found on a rooftop in Holborn and boasts a 27.5-metre outdoor pool.

Built on a Second World War bombsite, the pool rises above the busy streets of West London, surrounded by office blocks and residential buildings, with two sun terraces and an indoor pool for when the weather is poor.

www.camden.gov.uk/oasis
Address: 32 Endell Street, WC2H 9AG
Nearest tubes: Covent Garden, Tottenham Court Road

7 August
Learn to fly at Biggin Hill

The Biggin Hill School of Flying has been operating from Biggin Hill Aerodrome, in South London, since 1978, and offers regular flying lessons, using the runway from which the brave Spitfire pilots of the Second World War took off to fight in the Battle of Britain.

The school uses various light aircraft, and if you're feeling particularly adventurous — and have deep pockets — you can also take lessons in flying a Robinson R22 Helicopter.

www.bigginhillschoolofflying.com
Nearest rail: Hayes

8 August
Take a London Duck Tour

Huge yellow ducks stalk the streets around Waterloo Station, hunting for a suitable location to splash down ramps into the river, and make their escape. But these ducks are not the feathered kind, but 'DUKWS' amphibious vehicles, which previously served in the armed forces, and now act as tour buses for adventurous visitors.

Around 21,000 'DUKWS' vehicles were built, and were first used during the D-Day landings in Normandy. They were designed by the General Motors Corporation, in partnership with the New York yacht designers Sparkman & Stephens, and came to London as tour buses in 2003.

www.londonducktours.co.uk

9 August
Visit the Wildlife Garden at the Natural History Museum

The Natural History Museum's Wildlife Garden is an urban haven for thousands of British plant and animal species in South Kensington. Divided into different areas, the Garden recreates seven different habitats, in order to attract different species and give them an opportunity to thrive.

The Garden has previously been home to dragonflies, moorhens, moths, butterflies, foxes, robins, marsh marigolds, primroses, lime, bees, and even sheep, and it is always abuzz with wildlife whenever you choose to visit.

www.nhm.ac.uk/visit-us/galleries/orange-zone/wildlife-garden
Address: Cromwell Road, SW7 5BD
Nearest tubes: South Kensington, Gloucester Road

10 August

PICK BLACKBERRIES ON WORMWOOD SCRUBS

One of West London's best blackberry-picking spots, 200-acre Wormwood Scrubs is is the biggest green space in Hammersmith and Fulham and one of the largest commons in London.

Probably most famous for being home to the Category B men's prison, which has hosted the likes of Keith Richards and Pete Doherty and was the setting for parts of *The Italian Job*, the Scrubs is also home to a pony centre.

www.scrubs-online.org.uk
Nearest tubes: East Acton, White City

Cycle the Lee Valley

One of London's best off-road cycling routes follows National Cycle Route 1 through the Lee Valley Regional Park from Docklands to Tottenham and beyond.

The route passes Victoria Park, the Olympic site and Walthamstow Marshes, using a mixture of canal towpaths and cycle paths, making a lovely day trip with refreshment stops at the Markfield Park Café, the Riverside Café and Tottenham's Ferry Boat Inn.

www.sustrans.org.uk

LEARN TO SHOOT WITH THE WEST LONDON SHOOTING SCHOOL

ON THE GLORIOUS TWELFTH

Traditionally one of the busiest days on the calendar, 12th August marks the start of the shooting season for red grouse, but if you're looking for something rather more humane, the West London Shooting School offers regular shooting lessons at their ranges in Northolt.

Established in 1901 by the Richmond-Watson family, the school moved to its present location in 1931, and is the country's oldest independent shooting school, known for its clay pigeon courses.

www.shootingschool.co.uk
Address: Sharvel Lane, West End Road, Northolt, Middlesex UB5 6RA
Nearest tube/rail: South Ruislip

14 August

Find Falkland House

ON FALKLAND DAY

The people of the Falkland Islands celebrate Falkland Day to remember the day in 1592 when the Islands were first sighted by Captain John Davis from his ship, *Desire*.

In London, the Islands have their own base at Falkland House, in Westminster, which is charged with raising awareness of the Islands, and often hosts showcases of Falkland Islands products and exhibitions of Islands-related art and photography.

Address: 14 Broadway, Westminster, SW1H 0BH
Nearest tube: St James's Park

13 August

Watch the birds at Rainham Marshes RSPB reserve

Rainham Marshes is an RSPB reserve on the north bank of the Thames estuary near Purfleet, an ancient landscape which was used as a military firing range for over a century until 2006, when it opened to the public as a nature reserve.

The reserve has a visitors' centre, and various boardwalks take visitors out across the marshes to see wild ducks in winter or breeding wading birds in spring and summer, as well as birds of prey and rare birds and one of the densest water vole populations in the country.

www.rspb.org.uk/reserves/guide/r/rainhammarshes/index.aspx
Address: Purfleet, Essex RM19 1SZ
Nearest rail: Purfleet

15 August

Eat at the India Club

ON INDIAN INDEPENDENCE DAY

The India Club is an authentic Indian restaurant on the Strand which is said to be a favourite of officials from the Indian High Commission across the road.

First opened in 1939 before moving to its current premises in the 1950s, the restaurant has not changed much in recent years, and offers a truly authentic Indian experience, up an unmarked winding staircase in an old hotel, just like in the backstreets of Old Delhi.

Address: 143 Strand, WC2R 1JA
Nearest tube: Temple

Watch the sunset at the Point

The Point, on the hill above Greenwich, is one of London's finest views. As the day draws to a close, its two benches are a popular spot, where dog walkers and locals can often be found gazing out from the edge of the hill, as the view drops away beneath them.

Above the gabled rooftops, Tower Bridge rises between St Paul's Cathedral and the office buildings of the City, framed by the London Eye and BT Tower to the west, and the towers of Canary Wharf to the east.

Nearest rail: Blackheath, Greenwich, Maze Hill

Visit Forty Hall and Estate

Enfield's Forty Hall is a grand Jacobean house, built in 1629 for Sir Nicholas Rainton, shortly before he became Lord Mayor of London. Today, the Hall is open to the public, and sits within a 133-acre country park.

The Hall was acquired by the London Borough of Enfield in 1951, and is home to the Enfield Museum Service, hosting exhibitions and historical displays in its fine rooms. Today, the park which surrounds the Hall is home to a modern vineyard, which is the first of its size in London since medieval times.

www.enfield.gov.uk/info/1000000121/forty_hall
Address: Forty Hill, Enfield EN2 9HA
Nearest rail: Enfield Tow, Enfield Chase

Go to the Proms

The Proms are an annual season of around seventy concerts stretching nightly from mid-July to mid-September. Since their foundation by Henry Wood in 1895, they have entertained millions of concertgoers at a price designed to make them accessible to everyone.

While the Victorian concerts were priced at the equivalent of just 5p, tickets to the modern Proms start at a still-reasonable £5, with around 1,400 tickets to each performance available to those who just walk up – or promenade – to the Royal Albert Hall box office on the night.

www.bbc.co.uk/proms
Address: Royal Albert Hall, Kensington Gore, SW7 2AP
Nearest tubes: South Kensington, High Street Kensington

Take a tour of Eltham Palace

Though a palace has stood in Eltham, in South-East London, since it was acquired by Edward II in 1305, it is the Art Deco adaptations undertaken by Stephen and Virginia Courtauld in the 1930s that really capture the imagination.

Visitors are invited to wander around the Palace, admiring the grand panelled Swedish Entrance Hall, with concrete and glass dome, the Courtaulds' private quarters, where they planned trips around the world, and the bedroom of their pet ring-tailed lemur, Mah-Jongg. The Art Deco features and the Tudor Great Hall, with its grand hammerbeam roof, make an interesting contrast.

www.english-heritage.org.uk/daysout/properties/
eltham-palace-and-gardens/
Address: Court Yard, Eltham, SE9 5QE
Nearest rail: Eltham, Mottingham

20 August

DINE IN THE ORANGERY AT KENSINGTON PALACE

Designed for Queen Anne by Nicholas Hawksmoor and Sir John Vanbrugh in 1704, the Orangery at Kensington Palace is a grand red-brick glasshouse once previously used in winter for storing plants and in summer for grand court cermonies.

No longer the preserve of royalty, the modern Orangery is a restaurant, set among beautiful lawns and offering champagne breakfasts, light lunches and elegant afternoon teas.

www.theorangery.uk.com
Address: Kensington Palace, Kensington Gardens W8 4PX
Nearest tubes: Queensway, Notting Hill Gate, High Street Kensington

21 August

Search for Butterflies in Roding Valley Meadows

A 140-acre nature reserve alongside the River Roding, the Roding Valley Meadows are a Site of Special Scientific Interest and are rich in wild flowers, making them a perfect habitat for a number of butterfly species.

The reserve has been known to attract kestrels and sparrowhawks, and also has its own herd of Longhorn cattle which sometimes graze the meadows.

www.eppingforestdc.gov.uk/

• •

22 August

Walk along Erith Pier

In Victorian times, Erith, in South-East London, attempted to style itself as an upmarket pleasure resort, with visitors arriving by paddle steamer to its deep water pier from Central London.

Today, London's longest pier still remains at Erith, rebuilt in concrete and offering the chance to walk out for 100 metres over the water and enjoy spectacular views of the surrounding industrial landscapes and Queen Elizabeth Bridge downstream. The pier is a popular spot for fishermen who have been known to catch sole and other sea fish in the summer months.

www.bexley.gov.uk/index.aspx?articleid=3178
Nearest rail: Erith

23 August

Play croquet in Golders Hill Park

London has remarkably few designated croquet lawns, but the Golders Hill Park section of Hampstead Heath is home to two formal half-size lawns, adjoining Golders Hill Park tennis courts.

A formal Hampstead Heath Croquet Club was formed in 2008, and welcomes players of all ages, or non-members can hire the equipment directly from the court attendants for a small fee.

www.hampsteadheathcroquetclub.org.uk/
Address: West Heath Avenue entrance to Golders Hill Park
Nearest tube: Golders Green

24 August

Admire the flowers at the Churchill Arms

The Churchill Arms, in Kensington, is a traditional pub marked in summer by its beautiful award-winning floral displays. The beauty of the exterior is matched inside with a bar packed full of photographs, memorabilia and odds and ends.

The pub claims to be the first in Britain to serve Thai food, when landlord Gerry O'Brien decided to team up with a Thai cook after he took the pub over in 1985. It continues to do a roaring trade serving cheap, good food in ample portions.

www.fullers.co.uk/rte.asp?id=4&itemid=60&task=View
Address: 119 Kensington Church Street, W8 7LN
Nearest tube: Notting Hill Gate

25 August

Tour the Palace of the Bishops of London

The site of Fulham Palace, in West London, has been owned by the Bishops of London for more than a thousand years, and it was a summer retreat for more than a hundred bishops from the 11th century until they finally left in the 1970s.

Today, the Tudor Palace is a Grade I-listed building and is open to the public as a museum, with a separate tea room in the former Drawing Room, and also offers an opportunity to wander in the Bishops' Botanical Gardens.

www.fulhampalace.org
Address: Fulham Palace, Bishop's Avenue, SW6 6EA
Nearest tube: Putney Bridge

THINGS TO DO TODAY:

26 August

EMBRACE VILLAGE LIFE ON RICHMOND GREEN

Of the many villages of South-West London, Richmond is perhaps one of the most famous, and has its own village green – Richmond Green – surrounded by houses and pubs and home to two cricket teams.

Originally connected to the Old Deer Park, the green is still a centre for village life in Richmond, and is a lovely spot for a summer evening, with some great pubs.

Nearest tube: Richmond

August

27 August

TAKE A TRIP ON THE LONDON WATERBUS

In summer, waterbuses cruise the Regent's Canal between Camden and Little Venice up to eight times a day, for a 50-minute trip on one of four converted narrow boats, three on the National Register of Historic Ships.

The route passes through London Zoo – where birds can be seen flying inside Snowdon Aviary – and the 200-year-old Maida Hill tunnel, and return passage is available.

www.londonwaterbus.co.uk

28 August
Visit Osterley Park

Probably London's best preserved country estate, Osterley Park consists of a large manor house, situated at the heart of 357 acres of parkland and gardens. Today, it is are managed by the National Trust and is open to the public in the summer months.

The house we see today was created by architect and designer Robert Adam for the Child family, and both it and the gardens were completed in the late 18th century, on the site of an earlier manor.

www.nationaltrust.org.uk/main/w-osterleypark
Address: Jersey Road, Isleworth, Middlesex TW7 4RB
Nearest rail: Osterley

29 August
Remember Bellot

An obelisk stands beside the Old Royal Naval College in Greenwich to commemorate Frenchman Joseph Rene Bellot, who died on the second of two unsuccessful expeditions to try to rescue Sir John Franklin.

Franklin had undertaken an expedition trying to find a water route around the North side of the American continent, and during a recovery expedition Bellot was separated from the rest of the group, and died after falling through the ice in the Wellington Channel.

Nearest DLR: Greenwich

30 August
Admire the view that inspired Turner

The Angel in Rotherhithe is the site of one of the oldest public houses in Southwark, with an earlier pub built in the 15th century, to serve the monks of Bermondsey Priory. It was on the riverside terrace here that J. M. W. Turner observed the *Temeraire* being tugged to her last berth to be broken up in 1838, inspiring the painting which hangs in the National Gallery.

The ship itself was a celebrated gunship that had fought in Nelson's fleet at the Battle of Trafalgar in 1805, and you can still sit in the spot where Turner sat, watch the river traffic and enjoy an unrivalled view back down towards Tower Bridge, City Hall and the centre of London.

Address: Bermondsey Wall East, Rotherhithe, London SE16 4NB
Nearest tubes: Bermondsey, Rotherhithe

31 August
Row on the Thames

The best way to enjoy the Thames is in a rowing boat from Richmond Bridge Boathouses, which has occupied a prime spot on the banks for centuries.

Here, in late summer, the Thames is sleepy thanks to Richmond Lock and Weir just downstream, and – for a reasonable price – rowers are free to pick their own way up the river past the grand houses at Ham and Marble Hill, and drift effortlessly back downstream.

www.richmondbridgeboathouses.co.uk
Address: 1-3 Bridge Boathouses, Richmond on Thames TW9 1TH
Nearest rail: Richmond

September

1 September

Sit in an alcove of old London Bridge

Though the modern London Bridge dates from 1973, in medieval times London Bridge was the only way to cross the Thames in Central London, and one of the most famous versions was completed in 1209.

Pedestrian alcoves were added in a 1760 refurbishment to allow users of the bridge space to sit and take stock during their journeys, and two of these were relocated to the eastern fringes of Victoria Park in 1860, following the 1831 destruction of the old bridge, where they now act as simple park seats.

THINGS TO DO TODAY:

2 September

Climb Monument

On 2 September 1666, London was hit by one of the most devastating events in its history. The Great Fire of London raged for four days and nights, destroying 13,000 homes and nearly ninety churches before it was finally extinguished.

The fire changed the face of London forever, and in the subsequent years, a 202 ft Monument was built on a spot close to the Pudding Lane bakery where it is believed to have started. Today it is open to visitors, who are invited to climb the 311 spiral steps to the Monument's observation gallery, and admire the views over the City.

www.themonument.info
Nearest tube: Monument

WATCH A FILM AT THE INSTITUT FRANÇAIS' CINÉ LUMIÈRE

Housed at the Institut Français, in South Kensington, the Ciné Lumière is a one-screen cinema which hosts screenings for a range of French films, often with English subtitles.

The cinema has 300 seats, and also shows other European and world cinema films, mixing together classics and new releases. Alongside this, it regularly holds special events such as premières, retrospectives and themed seasons.

www.institut-francais.org.uk
Address: 17 Queensberry Place, SW7 2DT
Nearest tube: South Kensington

VISIT THE LARGEST HINDU TEMPLE OUTSIDE INDIA

Neasden's **BAPS** Shri Swaminarayan Mandir London is listed in the Guinness Book of Records 2000 as the largest Hindu Temple outside India, built under instruction from His Holiness Pramukh Swami Maharaj.

The temple, which cost £12 million, is made of 2,828 tonnes of Bulgarian limestone and 2,000 tonnes of Italian marble. Visitors are welcome for guided tours.

www.mandir.org
Address: 105–119 Brentfield Road, NW10 8LD
Nearest tube: Neasden

Notes

5 September

Visit the Painted Hall

The centrepiece of the Old Royal Naval College in Greenwich is the Painted Hall, planned as a dining hall by Wren in 1698, and decorated by Sir James Thornhill with the theme of the triumph of Peace and Liberty over Tyranny.

Though Wren's building was completed relatively swiftly, Thornhill's work took 19 years to complete. Legend has it that he was so confident of his abilities that he said he should only be paid what his work was worth, and his paymasters held back from any form of payment for some time.

Eventually, however, Thornhill secured a payment of £1 a yard, and he went on to become George I's court painter, a fellow of the Royal Society, before being elected to Parliament and knighted.

www.oldroyalnavalcollege.org/the-painted-hall
Address: 2 Cutty Sark Gardens, Greenwich, SE10 9LW
Nearest rail: Greenwich

6 September

Get back to nature in Greenwich Peninsula Ecology Park

Perched on the side of the Thames about a mile south of the Millennium Dome, the Greenwich Peninsula Ecology Park is a four-acre wetland nature reserve which attempts to recreate a number of habitats in an urban setting.

The Park has two lakes, with raised walkways for visitors, and hosts a variety of wildlife including frogs, toads and newts. In spring and summer, the Park also has significant numbers of dragonflies, damselflies and butterflies.

www.urbanecology.org.uk
Address:Thames Path, John Harrison Way, Greenwich Peninsular, SE10 0QZ
Nearest tube: North Greenwich

7 September

Drink at the Nell Gwynne Tavern

You can be sure of an authentic pub experience at the tiny Nell Gwynne Tavern, on Bull Inn Court, off the Strand, as it is reputed to have a guardian ghost, who is keen to ensure it remains well treated, and − so legend has it − has driven out landlords who have attempted to change it too much.

Named after Charles II's mistress, it is almost hidden from the Strand itself, and as such usually manages to avoid the tourist crowds who patronise other pubs in the area, though perhaps the guardian ghost can also be thanked for this.

Address: 1-2 Bull Inn Court, Strand, WC2R 0NP
Nearest tubes: Covent Garden, Embankment

8 September

Crawl around a badger sett

At the north-western corner of Kew Gardens, where few visitors stray, the Royal Botanic Gardens have created an oversized badger sett among the trees, allowing humans to discover what life is like for badgers, in their homes beneath the soil.

Created in 2003, to complement the 20 real setts which exist within the gardens, the human version is an educational tool to help us all learn more about the life of the badger, and is open to all − it is even accessible by wheelchair.

www.kew.org
Address: Kew, Richmond, Surrey TW9 3AB
Nearest tube: Kew Gardens

9 September

Walk a section of the London Loop

Skirting around the outskirts of London, the London Loop is a 150-mile circular walking route which passes through some beautiful areas.

Often described as an 'M25 for walkers', the route means that you are never that far from a section of the path, which is divided into 24 manageable walks.

www.tfl.gov.uk/gettingaround/walking/localroutes/1164.aspx

10 September

Visit the Herne Hill Velodrome

There has been a velodrome at Herne Hill in South London since 1891, and it was improved for the 1948 Olympic Games when it was used as a venue for the cycling finals.

The 450-metre cycling track, with banking of up to 30 degrees at each end, was repaired again in the 1980s, with the help of a £1.5 million grant from the EEC, and despite questions over its funding and future since then, it still remains a popular venue, attracting cyclists on most days of the week.

www.hernehillvelodrome.com
Address: Herne Hill Stadium, Burbage Road, SE24 9HE
Nearest rail: Herne Hill, North Dulwich

11 September

Do some research at the Marx Memorial Library

The Marx Memorial Library, in Clerkenwell Green, began life as a school before getting involved in left-wing politics when it became the home of the socialist Twentieth Century Press.

The building took on a revolutionary zeal when Lenin edited a newspaper from an office there from 1902 to 1903, while exiled in London, and in 1933 a group of trade unionists, communists and Labour Party members decided to turn it into a memorial library to Karl Marx. The Library may be used for research, or visitors can take a guided tour.

www.marx-memorial-library.org
Address: 37a Clerkenwell Green, EC1R 0DU
Nearest tube: Farringdon

12 September

See what's on at Cafe Gallery Projects

Established in 1984 in Southwark Park, Cafe Gallery Projects is a small art gallery made up of three interlinked white rooms, with a beautiful attached patio garden.

The Bermondsey Artists Group, who run the Gallery, hold exhibitions, and offer art and craft workshops and occasional DIY gardening groups, to engage the local community with the space.

www.cgplondon.org
Address: Southwark Park, SE16 2UA
Nearest tube: Canada Water

13 September

Spend an evening with a ghostly grenadier

Each September supposedly sees a peak in hauntings at the Grenadier in Belgravia, reputedly one of London's most haunted pubs. The pub is situated on a private mews, and was used as an officers' mess during the Napoleonic Wars, with the cellar acting as a drinking and gambling den for the lower-ranking soldiers.

Legend has it a card-playing junior soldier was beaten to death one evening, and subsequently returned to haunt the establishment, with customers reporting chills in the bar, and one former policeman even reported seeing a cigar smoking itself in mid-air beside him. Although a crucifix has now been installed in the cellar to ward off bad spirits, they continue to be reported.

Address: 18 Wilton Row, SW1X 7NR
Nearest tubes: Hyde Park Corner, Knightsbridge, Victoria

14 September

Watch the crowds from the steps at St Martin-in-the-Fields

There are few places in London better for people-watching than the steps of St Martin-in-the-Fields, the striking church which overlooks Trafalgar Square. Here, at the very centre of London, the steps offer an insight into life at the heart of the nation.

The steps have many stories of their own to tell, as this was where Dickens' David Copperfield met Mr Peggotty & Martha Endell, and it was from here that *The Big Issue* was launched in September 1991.

www.stmartin-in-the-fields.org
Address: Trafalgar Square, WC2N 4JJ
Nearest tubes: Charing Cross, Leicester Square

15 September

Visit the RAF Museum on Battle of Britain Day

The RAF Museum at Colindale in North London is one of the best museums of flight in the world, with displays of the 90-year history of the RAF and showcasing over 130 different aircraft.

The Museum is on the site of the original London Aerodrome – used by pilots during the Battle of Britain – and tells the history of the RAF over five buildings, from the earliest balloon flights to state-of-the-art modern aircraft through artefacts, aviation memorabilia, art and photos.

www.rafmuseum.org.uk
Address: Grahame Park Way, NW9 5LL
Nearest tube: Colindale

• •

16 September

Find the Marc Bolan Death Tree

Former T.Rex frontman Marc Bolan died on 16 September 1977 when a Mini driven by his girlfriend American singer-songwriter Gloria Jones had problems negotiating a humpback bridge near Gipsy Lane in Barnes. Bolan was in the passenger seat and when the Mini hit a sycamore tree, he died instantly.

The site has been a site of pilgrimage for Bolan fans ever since and, in 1999 the T-Rex Action Group was formed, undertaking the formal maintenance of the tree.

Address: Queens Ride, SW13 0HZ
Nearest tube: East Putney

Ride London's free passenger ferry

London still has a free vehicle ferry service, chugging across the Thames between Woolwich and Silvertown every ten minutes during the day.

A ferry has crossed this route since the 14th century, and the free ferry has been in operation since 1889, and is still going strong, operated by TfL connecting the North and South Circular to complete the route.

Visit Samuel Johnson's house on his birthday

A man whose wit inspired this book, the author of the dictionary, the great poet, essayist, moralist, novelist, literary critic, biographer, editor and lexicographer, Dr Samuel Johnson lived at various addresses during his London life, but the one most associated with him is 17 Gough Square, off Fleet Street.

Today, the house is open to the public, and offers a fascinating insight into the life of the great wig-wearing depressive, allowing visitors to see various rooms, including the famous garret where he formulated his dictionary.

www.drjohnsonshouse.org
Address: 17 Gough Square, EC4A 3DE
Nearest tube: Temple

Wander in Bunhill Fields

London is so densely packed that often some of the wildest spaces, especially in the centre, are graveyards, and Bunhill Fields on City Road underlines this. Its name is supposedly derived from 'bone-hill' and four wild acres of a much larger graveyard remain, containing mainly burials from the 17th, 18th and 19th centuries, though it originally dates from Saxon times.

Bunhill was known as a dissenters' graveyard and the graves of many non-conformists are here, including John Bunyan, author of *Pilgrim's Progress*, poet and painter William Blake and Daniel Defoe, author of *Robinson Crusoe*. It closed following the Burial Act of 1852 and the final burial took place in January 1854. Today, it is preserved as a community garden and haven for both squirrels and lunchtime office workers.

www.cityoflondon.gov.uk
Nearest tubes: Old Street, Moorgate

Watch for spooks in the Morpeth Arms Spying Room

Directly across the Thames from the MI6 building in Vauxhall, the Morpeth Arms is a Grade II-listed pub, which was acquired by the Youngs Brewery in 1984.

The upstairs Spying Room, added after the Secret Intelligence Service moved in across the river, offers a unique vantage point to observe the building over a drink, with telescopes and binoculars to allow customers to watch the mysterious goings on over the bridge.

Address: 58 Millbank, Westminster, SW1P 4RW
Nearest tubes: Pimlico, Vauxhall

21 September

Become an anarchist at the Freedom Bookshop

Britain's largest anarchist bookshop can be found in Angel Alley in Whitechapel. The building has been the headquarters of Freedom Press, which runs the bookshop, since 1968, and the organisation has been based in the area for most of its history, having narrowly escaped the bombs of both the First and Second World War.

The shop stocks thousands of books, newspapers and pamphlets on all manner of topics, as well as magazines, periodicals and newsletters detailing the latest advances in anarchist and radical thinking around the world. It also serves coffee.

www.freedompress.org.uk/news/bookshop
Address: Angel Alley, 84b Whitechapel High Street, E1 7QX
Nearest tubes: Aldgate, Aldgate East

22 September

Fly a kite on Blackheath

Once a lonely stretch of grass where Wat Tyler gathered his forces before the Peasants' Revolt of 1381, and where highwaymen stalked travellers on the London to Dover road, today Blackheath is one of London's most popular kite-flying spots.

The heath covers more than 250 acres and combines reliable winds and a lack of overhead cables or trees to attract kiters from around London. It even hosts a Kite and Bike Festival in the spring.

Nearest rail: Blackheath

23 September

Visit the Japanese Garden at Peckham Rye Park

Opened in 1908, the Japanese Garden in Peckham Rye Park was built around an old pond and now features a series of stream-fed ponds, with Japanese plants and shrubs.

The park is noted for its Japanese maple tree, with rich red foliage at this time of year, and paler leaves in spring and summer, and also features a Japanese bridge, as well as a Japanese shelter, installed in 2005 at the southern end of the garden.

www.southwark.gov.uk

24 September

Drink beer at the Jamaica Wine House

London's first coffee house – Bowman's – stood in St Michael's Alley off Cornhill and counted Samuel Pepys amongst its patrons. The Jamaica Coffee House took its place in the 1670s, before later being rebuilt as the Jamaica Wine House, a City stalwart which is still open today.

Outside the attractive pub, a sign records that this was the site of 'the first London coffee house at the sign of Pasqua Rosee's Head 1652', a cryptic reference to a Turkish manservant who was one of the partners in the original coffee house.

www.jamaicawinehouse.co.uk
Address: St Michael's Alley, Cornhill, EC3V 9DS
Nearest tubes: Monument, Bank

25 September

Eat at the Viet Noodle Bar

In the heart of theatreland on Greek Street, Soho, the Viet Noodle Bar is highly popular with pre-show diners looking for a quick and reasonably priced bite to eat, served in generous portions and with a smile.

Tables are limited and at peak times diners often have to wait, but in this area that is a sign of a good establishment, especially when scores of restaurants adorn the main Chinatown strip just a short distance away.

Address: 34 Greek Street, W1D 5DJ
Nearest tube: Leicester Square

26 September

Visit the Twinings Tea Shop

Thomas Twining opened his tea shop at 216 The Strand in 1717, and it still remains on the same site nearly 300 years later.

Back in the day, tea was big business. By 1825, the family had amassed so much money from the tea business, they opened a banking branch, Twinings Bank, and in 1838 they opened a new banking house beside the shop at 215 The Strand to keep all their money in. Just a year later, Queen Victoria was on board, granting Twinings a Royal Warrant for their tea, and the right to supply it to her personally.

www.twinings.co.uk
Address: 216 The Strand, WC2R 1AP
Nearest tube: Temple

27 September

BUY FRENCH LITERATURE AT AU FIL DES MOTS

At the heart of the Petite-France area which surrounds the Institut Français in South Kensington, Bute Street is lined with baguette shops, French restaurants and French bookshops. Au Fil Des Mots is one such bookshop, with an excellent selection of French-language books by authors of all nationalities, including a strong range of French literature.

It's a great spot for Francophiles, and is authentic from the friendly 'Bonjour' as you enter the shop, to the month-long shutdown in August to head for the Riviera.

www.aufildesmots.co.uk
Address: 19 Bute Street, SW7 3EY
Nearest tube: South Kensington

28 September

See London's Roman Amphitheatre

Deep beneath the Guildhall Art Gallery is a series of walls which marks the remains of London's ancient Roman Amphitheatre, discovered during excavations beneath the Guildhall in 1988, and opened to the public in 1999.

Entrance is included with a ticket to the Art Gallery above, and informative display boards tell the story of Roman London and explain how the Amphitheatre fitted into the City.

www.guildhallartgallery.cityoflondon.gov.uk
Address: Guildhall Yard (off Gresham Street), EC2V 5AE
Nearest tubes: Bank, Mansion House, Moorgate, St Paul's

• •

29 September

Take tea in Bishop Howley's Drawing Room

Designed specifically for him by the architect S P Cockerell, Bishop Howley's Drawing Room at Fulham Palace was completed in 1814, and was used by the Bishops of London for afternoon tea from then until the Palace was vacated in 1973.

Today, it is opened to the public as a tea room, and retains many interesting features from the days of the Bishops, including a grand chandelier and a carved chimneybreast which once stood in Appuldurcombe House on the Isle of Wight.

http://fulhampalacecafe.org
Address: Bishop's Avenue, SW6 6EA
Nearest tube: Putney Bridge

30 September

Visit the Whitechapel Gallery

Founded in 1901, to bring art to East London, the Whitechapel Gallery was designed by architect Charles Harrison Townsend, and, despite expansion in recent years, it remains in its original Grade II*-listed home.

The Gallery still plays an important part in education and outreach with the local community, and, as well as hosting school groups, it also holds film nights, talks, courses, concerts for interested Londoners and there is also an excellent restaurant and café/bar.

www.whitechapelgallery.org
Address: 77-82 Whitechapel High Street, E1 7QX
Nearest tube: Aldgate East

October

1 October

Eat at the Regency Café

The Regency Café, established in 1946 in Pimlico, is a quintessential greasy spoon cafe on Regency Street in Westminster, housed in a beautiful building, which could easily be described as a design classic.

Populated largely by lunching civil servants and media stragglers from nearby Channel 4, it specialises in British staples, served quickly and at very reasonable prices. It also occasionally doubles as a set for various films and TV programmes, and memorably featured in a scene in 2004's *Layer Cake*.

Address: 17–19 Regency Street, Pimlico, SW1P 4BY
Nearest tube: St James's Park

2 October

See Gandhi in Tavistock Square

ON HIS BIRTHDAY

Mahatma Gandhi, the great Indian spiritual leader, visited London a number of times: as a student, he spent three years studying law at UCL and subsequently trained as a barrister, and he returned again in 1906 and 1909 for shorter visits. In 1931, he came again to attend a Round Table Conference in London on behalf of the Indian National Congress.

During his student days, he took dancing lessons, and struggled so much to find decent food that he joined the Vegetarian Society, and was elected to the committee of their Bayswater branch. He is now commemorated by a monument in Tavistock Square, which was erected in 1968.

Address: Tavistock Square, Bloomsbury, WC1
Nearest tube: Russell Square

3 October

Drink at Katzenjammers Bierkeller

ON GERMAN UNITY DAY

Lurking in the basement of the Hop Exchange in Southwark is Katzenjammers, a re-creation of a Bavarian Bierkeller specialising in the finest German beer and food.

The bar was opened in October 2009, and features staff in German costume, and regular live music. It can sometimes get a little rowdy with after-work drinkers in the evenings, but on the German Unity Day, that is all part of the fun.

www.katzenjammers.co.uk
Address: Hop Exchange, 24 Southwark Street, SE1 1TY
Nearest tube: London Bridge

4 October

Discover the Royal Academy of Music Museum

The Royal Academy of Music is Britain's senior conservatoire, founded in 1822, and it has been educating students for musical careers ever since.

The Academy's Museum at 1 York Gate is home to the stringed instruments and early pianos from the Mobbs collection, as well as paintings, photographs, drawings, prints, busts, furniture and other musical objects. It also hosts regular exhibitions and events, which include live demonstrations of the Academy's historic piano collection.

www.ram.ac.uk/museum
Address: Marylebone Road, NW1 5HT
Nearest tubes: Regent's Park, Baker Street

WATCH CABARET IN A TOILET

Housed in a tiny former toilet beneath Aldwych, Cellar Door has a capacity of just **60** and is open every night until 1 am.

The venue hosts regular live music and cabaret acts, and claims to have attracted Oscar **Wilde**, Joe Orton and John Gielgud in its previous incarnation.

http://www.cellardoor.biz
Address: Zero Aldwych WC2E 7DN
Nearest tube: Covent Garden

6 October

Design crockery at the Biscuit Ceramic Café

At the Biscuit Ceramic Café in Greenwich, the menu is not just about tea and cake. Visitors are invited to choose ceramic items – from teapots to vases – and cover them with their own designs.

Items are then fired in the Café's kiln and can be collected a few days later, or delivered to your home.

www.biscuit-biscuit.com
Address: 3-4 Nelson Road, Greenwich, SE19 9JB
Nearest rail: Greenwich

7 October

Grab a cuppa from a Cabbies' Shelter

The building of green huts beside taxi ranks in Central London was begun by the Cabmen's Shelter Fund in 1875, with the help of a group of philanthropists who were keen to keep cabbies away from alcohol.

Today, they continue to serve as a place for taxi drivers to rest, socialise, eat and drink, and, while the inside is strictly off limits to ordinary Londoners, it is often possible to procure an excellent cup of tea through a small hatch at one end.

8 October

Eat at the Blueprint Café

The Blueprint Café has had a prime position on the first floor of the Design Museum for more than twenty years, with staff working under the direction of Head Chef Jeremy Lee for most of that time.

The Museum's strong design credentials have a visible presence in the Café's design, with clean lines and well-presented food and drink, but the stunning views to Tower Bridge and Canary Wharf are also a big draw for diners looking for somewhere special.

Currently at Shad Thames, the Museum (and café) hope to relocate to the old Commonwealth Institute in Kensington by 2014.

www.blueprintcafe.co.uk
Address: 1st Floor, Design Museum, Shad Thames, SE1 2YD
Nearest tubes: Tower Hill, Monument

9 October

Visit the London Architectural Salvage and Supply Company

Housed in elegant Brunswick House, beside Vauxhall Bridge, is the London Architectural Salvage and Supply Company, which specialises in recovering beautiful and interesting architectural and interior details and offering them for sale on the open market.

The company acquired the building in 2004, and repaired damage inflicted by squatters. It is now used as a fascinating showroom for a unique collection of architectural and interior fittings from doorknobs and bottles to chimneypieces, with prices ranging from £1 to £100,000.

www.lassco.co.uk
Address: 30 Wandsworth Road, Vauxhall, SW8 2LG
Nearest tube: Vauxhall

10 October

Drink at Bar Cubana

ON CUBAN INDEPENDENCE DAY

Legend has it that Fidel Castro was once a shareholder at Bar Cubana, on Lower Marsh in Waterloo. So, there is no better place to celebrate Cuban Independence Day, sampling Cuban food and drink, and hoping that one of their regular live Cuban musicians will be playing.

The bar was set up – and is still overseen – by Phillip Oppenheim, a former MP, who once served as a government minister, and is still involved in trade with Cuba, importing rum and coffee from the country, as well as organising the Carnival de Cuba, London's annual Cuban Carnival.

www.cubana.co.uk
Address: 48 Lower Marsh, SE1 7RG
Nearest tubes: Lambeth North, Southwark

11 October

POP IN TO THE TRICYCLE THEATRE

Opened in 1980 in a converted Foresters' Hall, Kilburn's Tricycle Theatre is a bastion of the arts in North-West London, offering up a range of performing and visual arts, as well as regular cinema screenings.

The Tricycle prides itself on offering a culturally diverse programme, which reflects the local community, but should not be dismissed as a local theatre, as it is a worthy rival to the theatres of the West End.

www.tricycle.co.uk
Address: 269 Kilburn High Road, NW6 7JR
Nearest tube: Kilburn

October

12 October

Gaze at the stars at the HSS Observatory

From mid-September to mid-April, the Observatory of the Hampstead Scientific Society is open to the public on Friday, Saturday and Sunday, and – providing it is a clear night – visitors are invited to come and stargaze.

Found on Lower Terrace, a short distance from Hampstead Heath, the observatory uses a six-inch Cooke refracting telescope, dating from the turn of the 20th century, and is one of the few places in London where the public can go to observe the night sky.

www.hampsteadscience.ac.uk
Address: Lower Terrace, near Whitestone Pond, Hampstead, NW3
Nearest tube: Hampstead

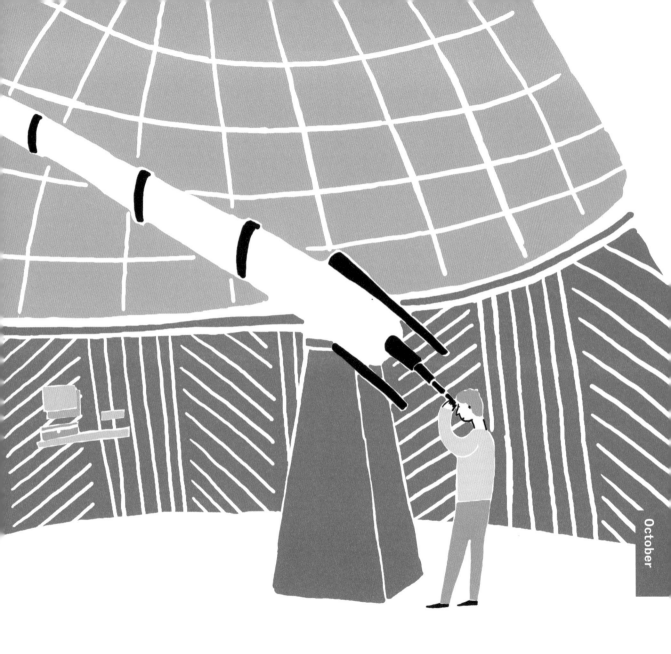

October

• •

13 October

Watch the deer rut in Richmond Park

Autumn marks the annual deer rut in Richmond Park, an ancient deer park which is still home to around 300 red deer and 350 fallow deer. The huge red stags and fallow bucks roar, bark and clash antlers to fight off their rivals, in their bid to attract females.

Patient visitors to the park at around dawn and dusk might be able to observe this display, one of London's most majestic natural phenomena. Calves are usually born in the summer, when they are protected from hordes of onlookers by the long grass.

www.royalparks.org.uk

• •

14 October

Seek out Severndroog Castle

Severndroog Castle is a folly which was built in 1784 as a memorial to William James of the East India Company to commemorate the 'conquest of the castle of Severndroog off the coast of Malabar' in the 1760s. The 63 ft-high Gothic folly it is on English Heritage's 'Buildings at Risk' register.

The Severndroog Castle Building Preservation Trust was formed in 2003 to save the castle from sale to private developers, and became a charity in 2008. It plans to restore the castle and open it as a café and educational space, with a viewing platform for visitors.

www.severndroogcastle.org.uk
Address: Castle Wood, Shooters Hill, SE18 3RT
Nearest rail: Woolwich Arsenal

• •

15 October

Play Mini Golf in Hither Green

Opened in January 2010, The Green Indoor Mini Golf is an 18-hole mini golf course owned by professional bridge player Nick Sandqvist.

The course is London's first competition indoor mini golf course, with regulation holes using Swedish felt, and has hosted a number of competitions in the sport.

www.wix.com/jwr20000/the-green-indoor-mini-golf
Address: Desvignes Drive, Off Hither Green Lane, Lewisham, SE13 6UR
Nearest rail: Hither Green

16 October

Wander in Westminster Hall

On the night of 16 October 1834, the medieval Palace of Westminster caught fire. As the building burned, Lord Althorp cried out: 'Damn the House of Commons, let it blaze away; but save, oh save the Hall.' On the Prime Minister's orders, the Hall was able to be saved, as it was when fires threatened it during the Blitz. As a result the Hall today looks much as it did in medieval times.

The public are free to enter the Hall and see the venue of the trials of Charles I, the only king of England to be sentenced to death, Sir Thomas More, and Sir William Wallace. The Hall has hosted also speeches by Nelson Mandela and the Pope.

www.parliament.uk
Nearest tube: Westminster

17 October

Visit Abney Park Cemetery

Originally an area of parkland laid out by Lady Mary Abney during the 18th century, Stoke Newington's Abney Park was later a Quaker school for girls before it was converted into a cemetery in the mid-19th century.

Created to alleviate overcrowding in Central London graveyards, it covers 32 acres and is surrounded by fairly built-up areas. There is a real feeling of wilderness in some parts, where small paths pick their way between tumbledown tombs.

www.abney-park.org.uk
Address: Abney Park, Stoke Newington High Street, N16 0LH
Nearest rail: Stoke Newington

18 October

Take a walk along the Thames Path

ST LUKE'S LITTLE SUMMER

For centuries, the days around St Luke's Day have been known as St Luke's Little Summer, offering one last chance to get outside before the winter closes in, and an ideal opportunity to get out and enjoy a stretch of the Thames Path.

While the full path stretches 180 miles from the Thames Barrier to the river's source in Gloucestershire, the stretch through London to the M25 near Staines, is the capital's finest walking route, taking walkers from the industrial heartlands around Woolwich, through the World Heritage Sites of Greenwich and Westminster, and on towards the green parkland of Richmond and Hampton Court beyond.

www.nationaltrail.co.uk/thamespath

WATCH LIVE ACTS AT THE TROUBADOR

Earls Court's Troubador Café is an original 1950s coffee house with a live music club downstairs, which, since opening in 1954, has hosted countless gigs, including those by Jimi Hendrix, Joni Mitchell, Bob Dylan and Paul Simon.

Upstairs, the attractive interior hosts diners and those drinking soft and alcoholic drinks until midnight, while downstairs the club offers a varied programme of music, performance and poetry.

www.troubadour.co.uk
Address: 263–267 Old Brompton Road, SW5 9JA
Nearest tube: West Brompton

20 October

Go climbing at the Castle Climbing Centre

The Castle Climbing Centre is housed in an old Victorian water pumping station in Stoke Newington and is officially the most visited climbing centre in the country.

For those who know nothing of climbing, they offer a Standard Taster Session for £20, and more experienced climbers can take advantage of 450 routes serviced by more than 90 ropes. The Castle even sometimes has an in-house DJ to climb to.

www.castle-climbing.co.uk
Address: Green Lanes, N4 2HA
Nearest tube: Manor House

THINGS TO DO TODAY:

21 October

Drink with Horatio Nelson at the Trafalgar Tavern

ON TRAFALGAR DAY

Built in the year Queen Victoria came to the throne, the Trafalgar Tavern was once at the forefront of Britain's naval history, attracting high-profile visitors such as William Ewart Gladstone, who dined here on whitebait with his Cabinet ministers in an annual tradition.

While there are other great pubs in the area, the Trafalgar Tavern's riverside setting beside the Old Royal Naval College is unrivalled, and allows visitors to enjoy a drink by the Thames, overlooked by a statue of Horatio Nelson.

Address: Park Row, Greenwich, SE10 9NW
Nearest rail: Greenwich, Maze Hill

22 October

Watch a film at the Phoenix

The Phoenix Cinema, in East Finchley, is believed to be the oldest purpose-built cinema in the country, dating back to 1910.

Saved from demolition in 1985, the interior retains its distinctive features and vaulted ceiling, and it is now managed by the Phoenix Cinema Trust, showing a range of classic and new films.

www.phoenixcinema.co.uk
Address: 52 High Road, East Finchley, N2 9PJ
Nearest tube: East Finchley

23 October

Visit the Canal Museum

The London Canal Museum is situated beside the Regent's Canal and opened in 1992, charting the history of the capital's inland waterways from the 18th century to the present day.

Housed in an old warehouse once used by an ice-cream entrepreneur to store ice imported from Norway, the Museum also offers occasional boat trips through the nearby Islington Tunnel.

www.canalmuseum.org.uk
Address: 12–13 New Wharf Road, N1 9RT
Nearest tube: King's Cross

24 October

Watch a hearing at the Supreme Court

In 2009, the UK's first Supreme Court was opened, opposite the Houses of Parliament in Parliament Square. Visitors are welcomed to the court, where it is possible to sit in the courtrooms and hear some of the finest legal minds in the country make their cases.

Entry is free, and as well as the courtrooms, there is also an exhibition on the work of the Supreme Court in the basement, and a café which is open to the public.

www.supremecourt.gov.uk
Address: Parliament Square, SW1P 3BD
Nearest tubes: Westminster, St James's Park

25 October

Eat at the Portrait Restaurant

Situated 92 feet above ground level on the top floor of the National Portrait Gallery, the Portrait Restaurant is a unique spot, popular with lunchtime and pre-theatre crowds.

The 80-seat restaurant offers stunning views over the National Gallery towards Nelson's Column and Big Ben.

www.npg.org.uk
Address: St Martin's Place, WC2H 0HE
Nearest tubes: Charing Cross, Leicester Square

26 October

Have a Martini at Duke's Bar

The bartenders at Duke's Hotel, on St James's Place, pride themselves on their reputation for serving some of the world's best Martinis.

Duke's was a popular haunt of James Bond creator Ian Fleming, and the hotel claims his visits were the inspiration for the fictional spy's preference for a Martini 'shaken, not stirred'.

www.dukeshotel.com
Address: St James's Place, SW1A 1NY
Nearest tube: Green Park

• •

27 October

DISCOVER YOUR FUTURE AT MYSTERIES

At the Mysteries shop in Covent Garden, they've been indulging in all sorts of New Age ideas since 1982, and they're still going strong, offering psychic readings, classes in creative mediumship, reiki and tarot, and a range of books and other things.

Join the likes of Naomi Campbell and Alanis Morrisette who have previously visited Mysteries, and start your year knowing what's around the corner other than a tall, dark stranger ...

The shop is open daily, with rather mysterious opening hours (Mondays, 10.02 – 18.55 etc).

www.mysteries.co.uk
Address: 9–11 Monmouth Street, Covent Garden, WC2H 9DA
Nearest tubes: Covent Garden, Tottenham Court Road, Leicester Square

Hunt for body snatchers at The Rising Sun

Legend has it that Victorian body snatchers once drank in The Rising Sun, on Cloth Fair, before going on bodysnatching raids to nearby St Bartholomew's Hospital. Some say that when they failed, pub regulars began to go missing.

Various ghosts are said to haunt the premises, and a nearby plague pit, with former staff reporting ghostly happenings and an eerie feeling on the stairs.

Address: 38 Cloth Fair, EC1A 7JQ
Nearest tube: Farringdon

29 October

See inside the stables of the Household Cavalry

Located within the grand Horse Guards buildings on Whitehall, the Household Cavalry Museum tells the story of the regiment and their work protecting the monarchy for nearly 350 years.

Visitors also get a behind-the-scenes look at the working block where the regiment's horses are stabled, to see them being groomed, watered and saddled ready for duty.

www.householdcavalrymuseum.co.uk
Address: Horse Guards, Whitehall, SW1A 2AX
Nearest tubes: Charing Cross, Westminster, Embankment

30 October

Drink at The Flask, Highgate

A beautiful 15th-century village inn in Highgate, North London, The Flask is a pleasant spot at any time of the year, but in autumn its low ceilings and dark-wood features make it a cosy spot.

Like seemingly every pub in the area, the highwayman Dick Turpin is said to have visited, and on cold evenings it is easy to imagine him propping up the bar planning his next daring stagecoach heist on the once rural surrounding roads.

Address: 77 Highgate West Hill, Highgate, N6 6BU
Nearest tubes: Highgate, Archway

31 October

Meet the scientists at the Natural History Museum's Cocoon

The Cocoon at the Natural History Museum is a unique exhibit, offering visitors the opportunity not only to learn about the team of scientists working within the Museum's Darwin Centre, but also to meet and interact with them, witnessing real specimens they are working on, and finding out about genuine scientific discoveries being made.

Opened in 2009, the Cocoon is at the centre of the new £78 million Darwin Centre, offsetting the clinical laboratories with a 200 foot-high, polished plaster structure which is filled with interactive exhibits to explain nature simply to non-scientists, including real-life caged scientists.

www.nhm.ac.uk
Address: Cromwell Road, SW7 5BD
Nearest tubes: South Kensington, Gloucester Road

November

Notes

1 November

Step inside 50 Berkeley Square, London's most haunted house

THE DAY OF THE DEAD

In Victorian times, 50 Berkeley Square was known as the most haunted house in London. It developed its fearsome reputation when a Mr Myers was jilted at the altar and became a recluse, living alone and only leaving his tiny room at night to walk by candlelight.

Later, following the death of a maidservant, owner Captain Kentfield was also found dead, his face twisted in terror, having tried to spend a night in the room, and two sailors who broke into the empty house died in rather mysterious circumstances. Since 1938, the building has been occupied by Maggs Bros, an antiquarian book dealer.

Address: 50 Berkeley Square, Mayfair, W1J 5BA
Nearest tube: Green Park

Notes

....
....
....
....
....
....
....
....
....

2 November

Set your watch by the Greenwich Time Ball

Since 1833, the Greenwich Time Ball has helped people to ensure their watches are correct, sitting atop the Observatory and rising halfway up its mast at 12.55 pm, then to the top at 12.58 pm, before falling at exactly 1 pm.

This was a vital service for ships in the area, to set their timepieces with exact Greenwich Mean Time, so that they could use a sextant anywhere in the world to work out their location.

www.nmm.ac.uk
Flamsteed House, Greenwich Park, SE10 9NF
Nearest rail: Greenwich, Blackheath

Browse at Hatchards, Britain's oldest bookshop

Established in 1797, Hatchards is the oldest bookshop in Britain, and one of the most famous in the world. It was also the venue for the first meeting of the Royal Horticultural Society in 1804.

The shop was started in 1797 by John Hatchard, and was granted a Royal Warrant by George III. Since then, it has attracted a range of customers including Queen Charlotte, Benjamin Disraeli, the Duke of Wellington, William Gladstone, Cecil Rhodes, Rudyard Kipling, Oscar Wilde and Lord Byron.

www.hatchards.co.uk
Address: 181 Piccadilly, W1J 9LE
NAddress: earest tubes: Piccadilly Circus, Green Park

4 November

Attend a service at St Paul's Cathedral

The evensong service is held at St Paul's Cathedral every day, allowing visitors of all faiths access to inside London's famous Cathedral, to see it as it was meant to be seen.

On most days, the service is led by the Cathedral Choir, made up of 30 choir boys, 8 probationers, who will later become full choristers, and 12 professional adult singers. The cathedral's amazing acoustics make for a magical experience, especially as the nights draw in.

www.stpauls.co.uk
Address: St Paul's Churchyard, EC4M 8AD
Nearest tube: St Paul's

5 November

Celebrate Bonfire Night

There are scores of Bonfire Night celebrations around London each November, remembering the failed gunpowder plot which sought to kill James I, and the death of Catholic Guy Fawkes.

Some of the biggest are at Blackheath, Victoria Park and Battersea, but, if you are looking for something on the night itself, the Westway Development Trust's annual event in Maxilla Garden is usually a good bet, with a giant bonfire featuring guys created by local schoolchildren.

6 November

Catch a Routemaster bus

Original Routemaster buses still operate on two routes in Central London, with both the Number 9 and the Number 15 operating every day between the Royal Albert Hall and Tower Hill.

Riders simply hop on at the back and wait for the conductor to come and collect the fare. It is a fantastic way to enjoy the nostalgia of the old buses while only paying the usual fare.

7 November

Search for Fagin's lair

In Charles Dickens' *Oliver Twist*, the criminal Fagin bases his gang of youths in a lair off Saffron Hill, where 18th-century tenements became an infamous rookery, packed with thieves and vagabonds, and were off limits to officers of the law.

Today, the hill in Clerkenwell has lost some of its original character, but, as you walk along it on a dark November night, you can still imagine the young pickpockets running up and down, off to do Fagin's bidding in the rich streets of the City.

Address: Saffron Hill, Clerkenwell, EC1N 8QX
Nearest tube: Farringdon

....

....

....

....

....

....

....

....

8 November

Explore the V&A Cast Courts

A highlight of any visit to the Victoria and Albert Museum, the V&A Cast Courts take up a pair of huge rooms, displaying plaster casts of some of the world's great architectural and sculptural masterpieces.

Collected since the opening of the space in 1873, many of the casts have stood the test of time and pollution better than many originals, and offer an amazing showcase, displaying Michelangelo's David alongside the pulpit from Pisa Cathedral, and a portal Cathedral of Santiago de Compostela in Spain.

www.vam.ac.uk
Address: Cromwell Road, SW7 2RL
Nearest tube: South Kensington

9 November

Watch Fijian fish at the Horniman Museum Aquarium

The Horniman Museum, on top of Forest Hill, houses many hidden delights, and one of the most unexpected is the excellent aquarium in its basement, which was opened in 2006 following an extensive refurbishment.

Visitors are offered the chance to immerse themselves in the underwater worlds of tropical Fijian coral reefs, British pond life, tidal rockpools, a mangrove swamp, and an area based on the South American rainforest.

www.horniman.ac.uk
100 London Rd, Forest Hill, SE23 3PQ
Nearest rail: Forest Hill

DRINK AT THE STAFFORD'S AMERICAN BAR

The American Bar at the Stafford Hotel dates back to the 1930s, when rich American tourists began arriving en masse by ocean liner. Since the 1970s, it has become more famous for the thousands of personal gifts that guests have left for the hotel, which now cover the bar's interior.

The tradition began, we are told, when the walls were so bare that an American guest gave the head barman a small wooden American eagle. This was duly followed by an eskimo, given by a Canadian, and a kangaroo, given by an Australian.

Today, the bar is covered with yacht-club flags, signed photographs and historical artefacts. These are kept alongside glasses which various Royals have used on their visits and model aircraft from pilots who drank at the bar during the Second World War.

www.kempinski.com/en/london
Address: St James's Place, SW1A 1NJ
Nearest tube: Green Park

Remember the Glorious Dead at the Cenotaph

On the day of the armistice that ended World War I, London gathers in a service at the Cenotaph at 11 am to remember those who lost their lives.

The monument to the dead, which stands on Whitehall, was designed in Portland stone by the imperial architect Sir Edwin Lutyens, and finished in 1920. It is a Grade I-listed structure, and bears no decoration, except a carved wreath on each end and the words 'The Glorious Dead', chosen by Rudyard Kipling.

Address: Whitehall, Westminster, SW1A 2BX
Nearest tubes: Charing Cross, Embankment

Kick through the leaves in Ruislip Woods

Traditionally, the days around Martinmas, in mid-November, offer the final warm spell before winter sets in, so it's a good idea to get out of the house, for one last chance to enjoy the outdoors before returning inside for winter hibernation.

Today is a good autumnal day to see the leaves fall at Ruislip Woods, in North-West London, the biggest area of woodland inside Greater London. The woods are famous for their oak trees, ponds, streams and marshes, and can be accessed by tube from the Metropolitan and Piccadilly lines.

www.ruislipwoods.co.uk

Take a tour of Toynbee Hall

Toynbee Hall, in Whitechapel, is a settlement house founded in 1884 by Samuel Barnett and his wife Henrietta. The aim of the house was to arrange for rich and poor in society to live more closely together, and volunteer middle-class settlement workers came to live in one of London's poorest urban areas to serve local people.

Celebrated residents included Clement Attlee and William Beveridge, two of the most famous social reformers of their generation. Visitors are welcome to take a self-guided tour of the Hall during office hours.

www.toynbeehall.org.uk
Address: 28 Commercial Street, E1 6LS
Nearest tubes: Aldgate East, Whitechapel

14 November

Explore Chislehurst Caves

Chislehurst Caves are a 22-mile system of tunnels dug over the course of nearly eight hundred years between the 13th and 19th centuries, as chalk and flint mines. Today, they are open to the public for interesting subterranean tours five days a week.

Since they stopped being used as mines, they have been used variously as an ammunition depot, an air-raid shelter, a music venue used by Status Quo, Jimi Hendrix, Pink Floyd, Led Zeppelin, The Rolling Stones and David Bowie, a mushroom factory and a set for the filming of *Dr Who*, so the guides are not short of stories to tell.

www.chislehurst-caves.co.uk
Address: Caveside Close, Old Hill, Chislehurst, Kent BR7 5NL
Nearest rail: Chislehurst

15 November

Learn about the Order of St John

The Museum of the Order of St John reopened in late 2010 after extensive renovations at its base in St John's Gate, originally the entrance to the former Priory of the Knights of St John in Clerkenwell. Through various displays it recounts the history of the Knights from their foundation in Jerusalem in 1099 to their modern role with the St John Ambulance.

The priory was the English base of the Knights from the 1140s, and the Museum follows them from their base in Jerusalem to Cyprus, then Rhodes, and more recently Malta. The Gate, meanwhile, also has an interesting history, and it was here that Dr Samuel Johnson was given his first job in London, writing reports for *The Gentlemen's Magazine*.

www.museumstjohn.org.uk
Address: St John's Gate, St John's Lane, Clerkenwell, EC1M 4DA
Nearest tube: Farringdon

Search for nautical novels at Maritime Books

Situated on Royal Hill in Greenwich, Maritime Books is a specialist bookshop, home to books covering every aspect of naval and maritime history, including countless old, new, out of print, used and rare volumes of all sizes and shapes.

Originally established in North London in the 1970s, Maritime Books moved to Greenwich in 1984, setting up shop in Greenwich Market, before later settling on Royal Hill in 2005, and expanding to include related material such as prints.

www.navalandmaritimebooks.com
Address: 66 Royal Hill, Greenwich, SE10 8RT
Nearest rail: Greenwich

Ride the dodgems at the Namco Centre

Never the first choice for a great day out, the Namco Centre in County Hall is good for some things. After all, there are very few locations in Central London where you can partake in traditional activities such as riding dodgems.

The Centre has a number of nippy Italian dodgem cars, which are available to hire, as well as pool tables, ten pin bowling and arcade favourites, just across the Thames from the House of Parliament.

www.namcofunscape-londonevents.co.uk
Address: County Hall, Riverside Buildings, Westminster Bridge Road, SE1 7PB
Nearest tube: Waterloo

●●●●●●●●●●●●●●●●●●●●●●●●●●●●●●●●●●

18 November

Have a drink at the Royal Oak

The Royal Oak on Columbia Road is one of East London's prettiest pubs, situated on a beautiful street that survived the bombs which destroyed huge sectors of the surrounding area, and on Sundays it bustles to the sounds of the famous flower market outside.

For the rest of the week, it is a great pub with a flawless interior and exterior, which has attracted film and TV crews who have used it as a location for various productions over the last 50 years.

www.royaloaklondon.com
Address: 73 Columbia Road, E2 7RG
Nearest tubes: Old Street, Bethnal Green, Shoreditch, Liverpool Street

●●●●●●●●●●●●●●●●●●●●●●●●●●●●●●●●●

19 November

See what's on at the Brunei Gallery

Just a few minutes' walk from the British Museum, in the heart of the University of London, the Brunei Gallery was built with the help of an endowment from the Sultan of Brunei.

The Gallery was opened at the School of Oriental and African Studies in 1995, and hosts a range of artistic and historical exhibitions focusing on Asia, Africa and the Middle East, organised over three floors. It is free to visit and has a Japanese-style roof garden.

www.soas.ac.uk/gallery
Address: Thornhaugh Street, Russell Square, WC1H 0XG
Nearest tubes: Russell Square, Goodge Street, Euston

EAT PIE AND MASH AT F. COOKE

Trading from the same location on Broadway Market for more than a century, F. Cooke's Pie and Mash Shop has changed little over the years and still sells authentic pie and mash with liquor, cooked in the old-fashioned way.

The owner, Bob Cooke, was born above the shop and talks of the pie and mash trade with great pride, offering friendly advice to customers and stories about the history of the shop.

Address: 150 Hoxton Street, N1 6SH
Nearest rail: Hoxton

WATCH THE MOUSETRAP

The world's longest-running show, with 23,000 performances under its belt, Agatha Christie's *The Mousetrap* has been at St Martin's Theatre for more than 35 years, with a cast of over 350 actors and actresses appearing over that time. It marks its 60th anniversary in November 2012.

It first entered the record books in April 1958 when it became the longest-running show of any kind in British theatre, but the show isn't the only record breaker, with some cast members themselves in the *Guinness Book of Records* for their lengthy stints on stage.

www.the-mousetrap.co.uk
West Street, Cambridge Circus, WC2H 9NZ
Nearest tube: Leicester Square

22 November

See the London Stone

Legend has it that the London Stone, on Cannon Street, was part of an altar built by Brutus of Troy, the legendary founder of London. Its safety is said to be intrinsically linked to that of the City of London itself.

Now housed in a box behind an iron grille on Cannon Street, it is so old that no one really knows what its story is, although it is said to be the place from where the Romans measured all distances in Britain.

Address: 105–109 Cannon Street, City of London EC4N 5AD
Nearest tube: Bank

• •

23 November

Visit Stave Hill Ecological Park

Acquired by the Trust for Urban Ecology in 1988, Stave Hill Ecological Park is a 5.2-acre nature area, located on the site of Stave Dock in the centre of the former Surrey Commercial Dock.

The Park is now managed by the Trust, which runs frequent volunteer days, workshops and wildlife walks.

www.urbanecology.org.uk/ stavehill.html
Address: Timber Pond Road, Rotherhithe, SE16
Nearest tubes: Rotherhithe, Canada Water

• •

24 November

Climb the Beckton Alps

Late November can be spectacularly bleak and the 'Beckton Alps' is a great spot to embrace that. The highest point in Beckton, East London, the hill was formed from a century of toxic waste dumped beside the nearby gas works, which closed in 1970.

In the 1980s, the hill was landscaped and, for a while, was home to a dry ski slope, but that was closed long ago and subsequent plans to build an indoor ski slope floundered when developers simply couldn't overcome the massive contamination in the ground. Beautifully bleak and neglected, it offers views over thousands of grey rooftops towards Central London.

Nearest DLR: Beckton

Heat up at the Ironmonger Row Turkish Baths

Ironmonger Row Baths, on sleepy Ironmonger Row a short walk from the City, was built in 1931 and houses a 30-metre pool, a Turkish Bath and a gym.

Run under contract from Islington Borough Council, the Turkish Bath has a steam room, a series of three hot rooms of varying temperature, marble slabs for massage and an ice-cold plunge pool.

www.aquaterra.org/ironmonger-row-baths
Address: Ironmonger Row, EC1V 3QF
Nearest tube: Old Street

Browse the Atlantis Bookshop

Founded in 1922, the Atlantis Bookshop in Bloomsbury is London's oldest occult bookshop, specialising in books on magic, ghosts and spiritualism.

It is supposedly haunted by the shop's original owner, Michael Houghton, with modern owners claiming to have seen his tall figure, dressed in grey clothing, striding towards the back door.

www.theatlantisbookshop.com
Address: 49a Museum Street, WC1A 1LY
Nearest tube: Tottenham Court Road

Seek out the Prince Consort Lodge

The Prince Consort Lodge was built by the Society for Improving the Condition of the Labouring Classes for the Great Exhibition in 1851, in order to demonstrate how a model home should be designed. When the Exhibition was finished, it was dismantled and re-erected in Kennington Park.

When re-erected, it operated partly 'as a Museum for Articles relating to Cottage economy to which the public may be admitted'. While it is sadly no longer open to the public – operating as offices for the Trees for Cities charity – the interesting design and modern gardens can still be seen from outside.

Address: Kennington Park Road, SE11 4BE
Nearest tube: Oval

28 November

Drink at the Nag's Head, Knightsbridge

The Nag's Head, on the easily missed Kinnerton Street in Knightsbridge, is a fiercely independent pub overflowing with character, and full of local curios in its small front bar and tiny back bar.

Landlord Kevin Moran has banned mobile telephones, and is known to tell customers off for not hanging up their coats properly, but he is clearly very talented at running a pub.

53 Kinnerton Street, Knightsbridge, SW1X 8ED
Nearest tube: Knightsbridge

29 November

Wander the streets by gaslight

There are still around 2,000 gas-powered street lights in London, identifiable by their glimmering filaments and their dim lights, and offering added atmosphere in gaslit areas such as the Royal Parks, Covent Garden, Mayfair, and outside Buckingham Palace.

Pall Mall was the first street to be gaslit, in 1807, and in 1812 the London and Westminster Gas Light and Coke Company was formed as the world's first gas company to manage the lights.

30 November

Have a drink at the Tate 7th-floor bar

The Tate Modern's 7th-floor bar offers unrivalled views over St Paul's Cathedral and the City of London.

Seats are limited, but the bar is open to all, accessed by lift and open during Museum opening hours.

www.tate.org.uk
Bankside, SE1 9TG
Nearest tubes: Southwark, Mansion House, St Paul's

December

Buy a Christmas tree at Clifton Nurseries

On Christmas Day 1851, a couple took out a 90-year lease on a plot of land at Clifton Villas, West London, to begin a business. Today, more than 160 years later, the centre is still serving the local community, making it London's oldest garden centre.

Each December, the Nurseries embrace the season with gusto, providing Christmas trees for hundreds of homes, shops, offices, hotels and public spaces. They also stock a wide range of decorations, and even provide a Christmas tree decorating service.

www.clifton.co.uk
Address: 5A Clifton Villas, W9 2PH
Nearest tube: Warwick Avenue

Notes

....

....

....

....

....

....

....

Embrace the season at the Christmas Shop

It might seem like Christmas comes earlier and earlier each year, but the owners of the Christmas shop, in Hay's Galleria, have been celebrating every day for 20 years.

So, if you need to get started on your Christmas decorations, there is no better place to visit, and in December it is open every day.

www.thechristmasshop.co.uk
Address: Hay's Galleria, 55A Tooley Street, SE1 2QN
Nearest tube: London Bridge

Visit Avery Hill Winter Garden

Created by fertiliser entrepreneur Colonel John North, the Avery Hill Winter Garden dates from 1880, and its grand central Victorian hothouse contains tropical plants from around the world.

Now part of the University of Greenwich's Avery Hill campus, the building and surrounded parkland are open to visitors every day.

www.greenwich.gov.uk
Address: Avery Hill Park, Bexley Road, SE9

4 December

FIND THE SEWER GAS LAMP

The Webb Patent Sewer Gas Lamp was invented in the 19th century as a way to draw off smells from underground sewers, and can still be found in Carting Lane off the Strand. Its hollow design allows sewer gases to be vented from underground, operating day and night.

Over the years, the lane has been nicknamed Farting Lane, and some claim that the gases can be seen and even smelled in certain conditions. While the original lamp was almost destroyed some time ago by a reversing lorry, it has since been restored.

Address: Carting Lane, WC2R
Nearest tube: Embankment

6 December

Explore Brompton Cemetery

At its eeriest when the dark winter nights are closing in, Brompton Cemetery is a 40-acre graveyard in the heart of some of the country's most expensive real estate in the Royal Borough of Kensington and Chelsea.

The only cemetery to be owned by the Crown, it was opened in 1836 during the Victorian cemetery boom. It contains around 35,000 monuments, based around a central avenue and a magnificent chapel based on St Peter's Basilica in Rome.

www.royalparks.org.uk/parks/brompton_cemetery

5 December

Drink at The Lamb and Flag

Thought to be the oldest pub in Covent Garden, The Lamb and Flag dates back to at least 1623, and is one of the most characterful pubs in the area.

The cosy pub is now Grade II-listed, and the poet John Dryden was among its patrons. He was famously mugged in the alleyway outside, and the upstairs bar is now named after him.

Address: 33 Rose Street, Covent Garden, WC2E 9EB
Nearest tube: Covent Garden, Leicester Square

7 December

Play with toys at Hamleys

Serving Londoners with toys since 1780, Hamleys is Europe's oldest and largest toy store and is a leading authority on toys.

The Regent Street store, which opened in 1881, is famed for its Christmas displays, with seasonal spectaculars throughout the shop and a chance to meet Father Christmas.

www.hamleys.com
Address: 188–196 Regent Street, W1B 5BT
Nearest tubes: Bond Street, Marble Arch, Oxford Circus

Learn to ski at Sandown Ski Centre

Out in the London suburbs, Esher's Sandown Park Racecourse has its own dry ski centre. The centre consists of one 120-metre slope, serviced by a button lift, and four tiny nursery slopes.

It's not really on a par with a fortnight in the French Alps, but it is a perfect spot to put in a couple of pre-season lessons to learn the basics before jetting off on a winter holiday.

www.sandownsports.co.uk
Address: More Lane, Esher, Surrey KT10 8AN

Sit by the fire at the Holly Bush

On the top of Holly Mount, in the heart of Hampstead, the Holly Bush is a village pub which offers a warm welcome and an even warmer fire, providing a cosy spot to spend a winter's evening.

The pub has occupied its current spot since at least 1807, when it was converted from the stables of a house called 'The Mount', and nowadays its country-pub style makes it a popular haunt of locals, as well as those from further afield.

Address: 22 Holly Mount, NW3 6SG
Nearest tubes: Hampstead , Finchley Road

Admire the Christmas windows at Fortnum & Mason

Every December, the great stores of Central London compete to put on the best window displays, and attract shoppers in to spend their money.

The team at Fortnum & Mason spend months each year working away in secret in an attic room in their premises on Piccadilly to produce seasonal masterpieces, battling with the likes of Selfridges, Liberty and others to produce the year's best window display.

www.fortnumandmason.com
Address: 181 Piccadilly, W1A 1ER
Nearest tubes: Piccadilly Circus, Green Park

Hunt for gifts at Greenwich Market

Greenwich Market is one of London's best and has operated from the same marketplace in the centre of Maritime Greenwich since the 1800s.

At Christmas, it pulls out all the stops, and as well as the usual crafts, antiques, food and drink, visitors can expect mince pies, mulled wine and carol singers.

www.greenwichmarket.net
Address: Greenwich High Road, SE10 9HZ
Nearest rail: Greenwich

Go shopping on Columbia Road

Columbia Road, in East London, is famous for its Sunday flower market, but it also boasts many independent shops, with more than forty non-chain stores offering some good present ideas.

The Sunday Market owes its licence to the large Jewish community that once lived in the area, and, while Sunday is still the busiest day, it can be more pleasant to browse the shops when they are a bit quieter. In the weeks before Christmas, the traders also often offer late-night shopping evenings, with festive events, food and live music.

www.columbiaroad.info
Nearest tube: Bethnal Green

13 December

Sing carols around the tree in Trafalgar Square

Every year, the Trafalgar Square Christmas tree becomes the centre of London's Christmas celebrations, and various community groups organise a programme of Christmas carols to mark the season.

The carols take place in the evenings in mid-December, raising funds for charity and bringing tourists and Londoners together every evening in song. Proceedings start at around 5pm.

www.london.gov.uk/trafalgarsquare/events/xmas.jsp
Nearest tubes: Charing Cross, Leicester Square, Piccadilly Circus

14 December

Watch *The Nutcracker*

The English National Ballet has been staging productions of *The Nutcracker* for more than sixty years, and continues to do so annually at the London Coliseum.

Audiences continue to enjoy the seasonal tale of Clara, Herr Drosselmeyer and the Nutcracker doll, making it the company's most popular show.

www.ballet.org.uk
Address: London Coliseum, St Martin's Lane, WC2N 4ES
Nearest tubes: Charing Cross, Leicester Square, Embankment, Covent Garden

15 December

See the lights on Oxford Street

While Oxford Street can get unbearably busy in the weeks before Christmas, it is always worth a visit to see the annual display of Christmas lights which hang above the shoppers.

The traditional lights were introduced in 1959, and since the 1980s a famous person has been invited along each year to switch them on. Each year's lights have a different theme, and bring the Christmas spirit as the nights close in.

Nearest tube: Oxford Circus

....

....

....

....

....

....

....

....

....

....

16 December

SPEND A SILENT NIGHT AT DENNIS SEVERS' HOUSE

Every Christmas season, the rooms of Dennis Severs' house, in Spitalfields, are decorated with the sights and smells of Christmases past, making it a particularly special time to make a visit

The late American eccentric Dennis Severs acquired the Folgate Street house in 1979, and recreated a series of period rooms inside, telling the story a family of Huguenot weavers who might have lived there from 1725 to 1919.

www.dennissevershouse.co.uk
18 Folgate Street, Spitalfields, E1 6BX
Nearest tube: Liverpool Street

December

17 December

Listen to the choir at St Martin-in-the-Fields

Trafalgar Square's parish church is always the centre of seasonal celebration in London, adding a bit of community spirit to proceedings with its annual Christmas Appeal, some of which goes to the church's project for local homeless people.

The annual carol concerts at the church help to raise funds for the Appeal, and for various other good causes, and are a great way to pass a few hours, regardless of whether you wish to sing or just listen.

www.stmartin-in-the-fields.org
Address: Trafalgar Square, WC2N 4JJ
Nearest tubes: Charing Cross, Leicester Square

18 December

Visit the Sir John Soane Museum

In the depths of winter, the early dark nights can be depressing, but they are also a positive thing, for, when the sun sets at 4 pm, you can see the Sir John Soane Museum in twilight. Soane was an architect who spent his spare time pottering around the world acquiring interesting items, and he bought 12 Lincoln's Inn Fields, and the house next door, to store them all.

Celebrated for his work on the Bank of England and rooms at Number 10 and 11 Downing Street, when Soane eventually died, he had collected so much he arranged for an Act of Parliament to allow him to bequeath it to the nation, and it remains to this day, with items piled on top of each other with barely enough room to breathe.

www.soane.org
Address: 13 Lincoln's Inn Fields, WC2A 3BP
Nearest tube: Holborn

Get a turkey from Smithfield Market

Smithfield Market has been the centre for London's butchers for more than 800 years, and was originally a livestock market to which animals were driven from the villages around London to be sold. The turkey which Scrooge purchases in Charles Dickens' *A Christmas Carol* would probably once have pecked the ground at Smithfield.

Since 1852, it has traded in fresh meat, and still opens at 3 am each weekday to trade to both the public and wholesale buyers. In the weeks before Christmas the market does a strong trade in Christmas fare; it is still where some of London's best turkeys can be found, and in late December the market's Great Annual Turkey Auction can be a chance to pick up a bargain.

www.smithfieldmarket.com
Address: Smithfield Market, EC1A 9PS.
Nearest tubes: Farringdon, Barbican

Browse at Daunt Books, Marylebone

A perfect traveller's bookshop, Daunt Books, on Marylebone High Street, is a grand Edwardian bookshop, with a dark green and oak frontage and thousands of books inside, arranged by country.

The store is known for its long oak galleries and beautiful interior with William Morris prints and skylights, and it has been described as the most beautiful bookshop in London in the *Daily Telegraph*.

www.dauntbooks.co.uk
Nearest tubes: Marylebone, Holland Park, Hampstead, Belsize Park

Go ice-skating at Somerset House

At Christmas, the cobbled Edmond J. Safra Fountain Court at the centre of Somerset House is transformed into a winter wonderland, with a large ice rink overlooked by a huge Christmas Tree.

The 900-square metre rink is London's finest, and offers skate hire and marshals to look after struggling skaters. A skate here is an important part of the seasonal ritual each year for many Londoners.

www.somersethouse.org.uk/ice-rink
Address: Somerset House, Strand, WC2R 1LA
Nearest tubes: Temple, Covent Garden, Charing Cross, Embankment

22 December

Pick up a bottle at the Vintage House

Situated at 42 Old Compton Street, in the heart of Soho, the Vintage House is a family business, founded during the Second World War. The quintessential off-licence, it is excellently stocked, claiming to offer the world's largest list of malt whiskies.

During his time here, owner Malcolm Mullin has sold wine to The Beatles and cigars to Angelina Jolie, mixed with legendary London gangsters, been shot at, and had a front-row seat on all the goings-on in Soho for nearly forty years.

Alongside the whiskies, which are mostly to be found in a special room at the back of the store, the Vintage House also sells Armagnacs dating back as far as 1879, and an excellent range of fine wines, Cuban cigars, liqueurs and other spirits.

http://freespace.virgin.net/vintagehouse.co
Address: 42 Old Compton Street, W1D 4LR
Nearest tubes: Tottenham Court Road, Leicester Square

23 December

Buy chocolates at Charbonnel et Walker

Charbonnel et Walker has been a market leader in handmade chocolates since 1875, when Mrs Walker decided to work with Madame Charbonnel, an experienced chocolatier from the Parisien Maison Boissier chocolate house.

Today, the chocolates are sold from a shop on the Royal Arcade on Old Bond Street, and are even a favourite of the Queen, who has endorsed them with the Royal Warrant.

www.charbonnel.co.uk
Address: One The Royal Arcade, 28 Old Bond Street, W1S 4BT
Nearest tube: Green Park

24 December

Attend Midnight Mass at Westminster Abbey

The annual Christmas Eve service at Westminster Abbey is enough to make even the most hardened cynic feel seasonal joy. One of London's most atmospheric church services, it has attracted people from all walks of life to see in Christmas Day for nearly a thousand years.

The service usually begins at around 11.30 pm, but it is a good idea to arrive early to avoid the crowds who flock to spend Christmas Eve with the ghosts of Dickens, Darwin and Johnson, who are all buried below the floor.

www.westminster-abbey.org
Nearest tubes: St James's Park, Westminster

WATCH THE PETER PAN CUP

ON CHRISTMAS DAY

While you're relaxing at home on Christmas Day, wondering whether to get out of bed, down in Hyde Park the members of the Serpentine Swimming Club are preparing for a different sort of treat. Every year since 1864, they have come together for a 100-yard Christmas Day swim now known as the 'Peter Pan Cup', in reference to *Peter Pan* creator J. M. Barrie, who was a patron of the race.

The race kicks off at 9 am, and, while you are welcome to watch, it is only open to members, as to anyone who has not spent the time getting used to swimming in waters usually around 4 degrees centigrade, the shock could prove fatal.

www.royalparks.org.uk/peterpan_cup.cfm

26 December

Place a bet on the King George VI Chase

ON BOXING DAY

While only four horses ran the first meeting of the King George VI Chase at Kempton Park Racecourse, in West London, in 1937, today it is one of the most important chase events on the calendar.

Moved to Boxing Day – snow permitting – when the course reopened after the Second World War, horses have run off their Christmas dinners on the three-mile course on the same day ever since.

www.kinggeorgechase.com

27 December

Go on a tour with London Walks

The guides of London Walks are dedicated to their jobs, and organised walks depart every day of the year, in many different areas of London. They run special Christmas tours, alongside their usual tours of different areas of London.

London Walks has been running for more than fifty years, making it the oldest urban walking tour company in the world. It also tries to operate as a guides' cooperative, where proceeds are shared by guides.

www.walks.com

28 December

Drink at The Spaniards Inn, Hampstead

The Spaniards Inn, in Hampstead, was built in 1585, and was for many years a tollgate inn, forming the entrance to the Bishop of London's estate. The tollgate remains and traffic is reduced to one lane outside, often making it difficult to cross the road.

It is a beautiful spot, with cosy bars that have changed little since Lord Byron, Bram Stoker, John Keats and Karl Marx drank here. Many love The Spaniards Inn so much they cannot be torn away – even after their deaths – and a number of ghosts are said to roam the area, including a ghost horse who haunts the car park.

www.thespaniardshampstead.co.uk
Address: Spaniards Road, NW3 7JJ
Nearest tube: Hampstead

29 December

Find Thomas Becket's memorial

THOMAS BECKET'S BIRTHDAY

Born in Cheapside in the 12th century, Thomas Becket is a saint who is remembered on 29 December, the day he was brutally murdered in 1170.

Becket rose to become the Archbishop of Canterbury at the time of his death, and is canonised in both the Anglican and Catholic Churches. A sculpture by Edward Bainbridge Copnall can be found in the gardens beside St Paul's Cathedral, capturing Becket's final moments as he was murdered at Canterbury.

www.stpauls.co.uk
Address: St Paul's Churchyard, EC4M 8AD
Nearest tube: St Paul's

30 December

Drink wine at Gordon's Wine Bar

RUDYARD KIPLING'S BIRTHDAY

Found in the subterranean cellar of a former warehouse that was home to Samuel Pepys in the 1680s, and Rudyard Kipling in the 1890s, Gordon's Wine Bar was established in 1890, and is the oldest in London.

Founded by Arthur Gordon, the bar is still owned by a Gordon family, though the current clan aren't actually related to the originals. It only serves wines, with no beer or spirits available, and a range of cheeses and meats are on offer. On busy evenings, drinkers spill out into the alleyway next door, but by far the most appropriate place to drink in the atmosphere is in the cellar, lit by flickering candles.

www.gordonswinebar.com
Address: 47 Villiers Street, WC2N 6NE
Nearest tubes: Embankment, Charing Cross

31 December

Watch the fireworks over the Thames

As the year draws to a close, there is really only one place to be, as 250,000 people line the banks of the Thames to see in the New Year.

Every year, the Mayor of London hosts a fantastic fireworks display, with a soundtrack dominated by the bongs of Big Ben, as millions at home watch them echo around the world.

INDEX